In-Your-Face Human Relations

by
Jim Wilhelm

Table of Contents

Introduction

Let's get real! I'm tired of inconsiderate people, I'm tired of being cut off on the freeway, I'm tired of rudeness, and I'm tired of living in a world of selfishness. Stop thinking about yourself for once and help someone else. You'll be surprised how good it makes you feel. Regardless of what some may think, hard work, study and caring about fellow human beings will continue to remain the formula for success. There are no short cuts. It's not who you know and it's not luck. Stop pussyfooting around and acquire some Human Relations skills or you're going nowhere in this world! We all know technology rules the world, and that will continue, but when you do meet a person face-to-face you'd better be able to relate to them. If you don't know: what to wear, how to act, how to control yourself, how to put your ideas forward, how to impress, or what your values are, the odds are stacked against you succeeding.

What is this book?

This is an "in your face" book that will teach you how to get along with other people if you ever want to get your needs met. If it's made into a movie it will be rated "R," because of content and using plain English. It may not be politically correct and I won't use flowery language or a "fog index" to confuse you. I genuinely feel the time is now to stop beating around the bush and get down to Human Relations principles that will carry you through life successfully! This is Dale Carnegie's book, *How to Win Friends and*

Influence People, on steroids! When you've mastered the techniques in this book, you will be successful! It's a short course that tells it like it is and builds you up to the person you know you are inside and can be on the outside. Take these chapters to heart and conquer the world! It's only too late if you think it is!

<u>Who am I?</u>
My name is Jim Wilhelm, I've taught over 180 sections of Human Relations in 30 years of college teaching. I'm here to say that, we, as a people, are getting more selfish and rude every day and I'm tired of it! It's partly due to the speed at which we are living, the stress we are under, and certainly technology. We used to be up in arms when someone was talking on their cellphone in a restaurant or grocery store line. But we've become so desensitized; we accept rude behavior without thinking twice. The last time you sat in your doctor's waiting room, how many people were on their cellphones? I don't want to hear their conversation and I'm private and courteous enough to speak outside of earshot when my phone rings. There's an old concept called "courtesy." It is still a valid concept but we've simply lost sight of it. Our focus is on our own agenda and getting things done. The attitude that it's too time consuming to hold the door for someone or help them with a heavy load is wrong. Try thinking of someone else instead of yourself all of the time.

For instance, when I'm driving on the road in a 3500 lb. machine that can do major destruction, I pay attention. People multi-task while driving and feel they can do three or four things at once to save time while driving to work. We are not accountable for our actions anymore and look to blame someone else. Do we need to pass a law against texting and driving? Apparently so! Many states are passing such laws because people don't have sense enough to know the distraction danger. It's physically impossible to read your text messages and look through the windshield at the same time. I could never forgive myself if I hit a pedestrian because I wasn't paying attention while driving. Technology has re-wired our brains to where we want everything instantly. We have to text and read email the second we are alerted, so now people are walking into poles and off of curbs due to inattention. We are on call 24-hours-a-day with computers, cellphones, cameras everywhere recording our every move and stress is the result. Can you turn your computer off for the weekend? How about your cellphone? Most people can't. Try turning off the television news since the first few stories will only be about robberies, accidents, and crime in general, because mayhem gets ratings. It's totally depressing. So why is it that when a good deed hits the news channels, the "feel good" stories about it are overly emphasized? Because good behavior and caring about our fellow human beings is not the norm anymore! It's rare, and it shouldn't be. I saw a video on the recent California wildfires of a man rescuing a wild rabbit from the fire. Of course, the story went viral with such comments as "there are still good people in the world," "he's a hero," "he stopped and saved a life." Isn't that what we should be doing, helping others?

I saw where a college football coach was totally dismayed after his team had upset a higher ranked opponent and fans damaged the field and tore down the goal posts in celebration. He was amazed that everyone didn't expect to win and he wanted to instill a winning attitude as normal behavior rather than an aberration. We need to prepare to win, and then expect to win!

My credentials

Let's get credentials out of the way. I have a Bachelor's degree in Business, a Master's degree in Management, and a Doctorate in Education. Oh, and I've written three books. So what? If I can't learn how to deal with people and better my life then my education was a waste. Why am I writing this book? You don't need college degrees to write a book. Bob Dylan said "you don't need a weatherman to know which way the wind blows." Anyone can have a great idea. The key is to put the idea into action and see it through. I'm writing this book now because the time has come to correct our behavior. The world is more unstable than it has ever been. The Bulletin of the Atomic Scientists announced January 25, 2018, that they have moved their Doomsday Clock 30 seconds forward to "two minutes to midnight," or two minutes to "apocalypse." That's a wakeup call! How can we stop wars and live in peace when we can't even get along with our neighbors or our colleagues at work?

We need a grassroots movement of caring, sharing, and preparing for proper etiquette and how to treat one another. Help someone. Make others' lives easier so that they might benefit from your experience. Success breeds success!

Frustration and concern

I sense uneasiness in America because of our president's behavior. From the leader of our nation, we expect professionalism, decorum, tactfulness, and courtesy. Instead, we are learning that exaggeration, insults, name-calling, and bullying are becoming the norm for this administration. It makes us uncomfortable when a leader continually denies facts. Just saying something is true, doesn't make it true. There is no logic when there's a preoccupation to insult everyone who disagrees with you. The trend is to bull your way through with little regard to listening to others' input. It's a shame and this is proof that positive human relations are needed to reverse this boorish behavior. We need to end the "half-truths." A sitcom comes to mind as an example, when a man tells his friend, "I'm going to tell everyone your father spent time in prison." The man says, "My father was the warden." The friend then says, "I'm not going to say that part." Half-truths foster miscommunication and are actually lies. Don't get me wrong, *this is not a book about politics,* I'm simply pointing out that when leaders don't behave properly it makes us believe that it is okay to mimic that behavior. That's a dangerous message for society and for your organization.   It is hoped that the president settles in, tempers the damaging rhetoric and focuses on leading our country.

We know many ads nowadays are full of half-truths. It's a pity that we almost expect them to be deceptive and to make claims too good to be true. Think for yourself and check to see if facts back up claims. My pet peeve is watching a 'miracle' commercial that advertises that over two million people have bought their "fantastic remedy for what ails you." That means two million people could be wrong. Were that many people only one-time buyers? Or, is it a worthwhile product? Do your research and think for yourself! Let's be honest in our communication with people. We need to get back to treating our fellow human beings with courtesy and respect while making certain there's still room for healthy disagreement.

Regarding this scholarly work, I will cite research to demonstrate the validity of my writing. But, through my education and experience, I consider my opinions valid also. You won't have a problem separating the two.

As I approach retirement, it always amazes me when people think working for the same company for 45 years is something special. It is special if the person continued to grow and hold several positions throughout the years. I wonder if it's that special when a person has been doing the same job at the same company for that long? Were they in a rut? Did they put their mind in neutral for years and years, numbing out change and simply punching the time clock every day until retirement surprises them? Of course, retirement is to be celebrated because whether you've had the same job or nine jobs, you've paid your dues and worked for 40-45 years. Celebrate! You deserve it! I believe it's in the human psyche to want to move, to progress in life. One reason communism is so degrading to individuals is that there is no chance to elevate. They have no hopes and dreams because the state tells them what to do. The state takes the power of choice away from them. In the United States, I've never understood why a person would want to stay in a low-paying job for years and not progress. Some people say it's for security. It would seem to be the opposite of security because if they're paid so little then their job may be the first to go or to be replaced. Wake up! Go back to school, read, and train yourself. Broaden your horizons, in case you are laid off you can move to other employment. Or, if you simply tire of the work you can easily find employment elsewhere with your skill set. As individuals, we are like couples because if a couple's relationship isn't growing, it's stagnant and declining. If we find a job we like and don't progress or update our skills then change will kick us out the door and we'll be wondering what happened. Keep striving! Also, be aware of specialization. When you specialize in your job it may be difficult to find another job that fits that specialty. I know, I've been in that position. It's critically important to continually learn and make yourself more valuable. No one wants to be held hostage by their company knowing that if they leave they'll take a pay cut because they can't find that exact specialty elsewhere that they had mastered so well. Companies certainly don't do that on purpose. They want to be able to compete and lower operating costs in a dynamic environment, and a specialized workforce is more efficient.

If you use this book to level your dinner table so your vittles won't slide off, then don't cry to me when you don't get promoted, you fail at things and relationships, or you can't hold a job. It's the choices we make that determine our quality of life. We can choose to stay down and wallow in our shortcomings or stand up and do something that will make a difference to us and to the world. Choose to stand up!

What are you going to read?
This project is built around essentials needed for a relevant, satisfying life. Chapter 1 deals with Communication and Expectations. It is the basis for everything. If we can't communicate properly and let others know our expectations then we'll be relegated to living someone else's life. We will never get what we want. Chapter 2 is about Values and Ethics. Core values, set early in life, dictate our behavior towards everyone we meet, how we do our jobs, and how we live our lives. Attitudes also

evolve from our value system. Chapter 3 brings us to the all-important Self-Esteem and Positive Reinforcement. If you don't feel good about yourself you can't effectively help others. Self-esteem is a large part of our make-up and positive reinforcement can spur friends and family to reach their goals. Chapter 4, Motivating, is my favorite concept because without motivation you'll lack the will to get out of bed and accomplish. Motivation is internal and it derives from what we value and how we feel about ourselves. It's the pathway to goal accomplishment. The last chapter, Chapter 5, deals with Conflict Management and having Emotional Control. There are people we like and some who don't like us. That's called "living." To have a fulfilled life we must be able to control emotions but, unfortunately, those emotions can sometimes result in conflict.

Don't dismiss these ideas lightly by thinking, "Oh, I could never change that," or, "Management never listens," or, "That's the way it always is, there's nothing I can do." Look at individuals like Abraham Lincoln, Leonardo da Vinci, Wolfgang Amadeus Mozart, or J.K. Rowling, these people changed the world with great ideas, leadership, and music. We can too! When we change ourselves for the better, we change the world for the better. But it has to start with the individual.

Table of Contents (expanded)

Chapter One – Communication & Expectations
Communicate, don't dictate!

1. Communication

When all else fails, try communicating!

I teach in a community college where administration dictates many procedures and new programs to us. Some fail, because they don't get input from those of us on the firing line, the teachers. Administration may think they know best, but they are removed from the classroom and are clueless about what programs will succeed. Hey, if you haven't been in the classroom for years, then swallow your pride and ask those who are currently in the classroom! It seems so simple, but pride and ego get in the way. I'm wise enough to know my limits and if I don't know much about something then I'll find someone who does. For example, I don't know much about electricity so I won't try repairs myself because I might burn the house down. It is worth the time and expense to get an expert to do the work. It's not a pride thing with me, but I think it is with some managers. Good people can't perpetually overcome bad decisions by management. It catches up by losing good employees, losing sales, and costing the organization a lot of money in having to hire and train new employees. All they had to do was communicate with those who will be affected by the decision. Duh!

Another case in point, I once worked as an insurance adjuster and was suddenly called by the big boss (branch manager) to come work in Dallas to cover the territory. I respectfully questioned the order and said there would be no one in Lubbock to cover my territory and that the Dallas adjusters could more easily cover theirs. He immediately told me that he was the boss and that I was to work in Dallas. So I took the redeye into Dallas the next morning only to be met by my immediate supervisor when I arrived at the office. He asked what I was doing there and I told him. He said to take the next flight back to Lubbock. I ended up having lunch with the girls in the office and flew back that afternoon. Because of miscommunication and a manager's power play, it cost the company in wasted time, travel tickets, and not servicing the territory. The branch manager, at the very least, should have checked with my immediate supervisor or listened to me and gotten off his high horse. Another "duh" is in order!

Many managers say they don't have time to ask for input or to listen, so they simply issue orders. That works fine in the military when lives are dependent on decisive measures and teamwork. However, it doesn't work so well in the workplace. Employees want to know what is happening and to be asked their opinions. We all want to be valued and it is a form of validation to ask someone's input. It pays dividends for the company. We, as employees, know you care because you thought enough of us to ask for our advice! The end result being a better decision through more input and a boss that's respected for having asked. It's a win-win!

Good communication needs to be timely, also. What happens where I work and probably where most of us work is that when change is perceived as needed, it seems it has to be implemented almost immediately. There is very little notice and sometimes management doesn't understand what's involved but they pass it on to subordinates anyway which only makes it worse. It causes confusion and many questions go unanswered because management hadn't done their job properly. Effective communication entails thinking things through thoroughly and then disseminating that information to subordinates or colleagues in a timely manner. If training is useful, then time should be set aside to assist others. If the changes are rushed into service haphazardly, it leaves employees confused and bewildered. My college has a knack for implementing decisions quickly without much forethought and it just makes it more difficult for everyone. What's the hurry? Why the big rush? If time is taken to think the change through completely and consider where there might be possible problems, then employees are more likely to embrace the new software or policy rather than fighting it. Communication should be timely or it can actually waste time and can lower morale. In other words, make sure it works before you implement it, then communicate the information at the correct time and the chances of failure will be minimized. It is called "communication" for a reason!

There is no question that good communication can be hard to come by at times. Whether talking with a child, a spouse, your boss, a relative, or a client, clear and effective communication is required to get your needs met. And it must be practiced constantly.

***Wise men speak because they have something to say;
    Fools because they have to say something -- Plato

Communication is the Basis for Everything

Whether just before filing for divorce or before N. Korea launches a missile, TALK! It's called communication and it's never too late to communicate. I totally disagreed with Donald Trump when he said the time for talk is over with N. Korea. I guarantee, the time for talk will be over if they launch a nuclear missile, but until that happens (I hope it never does), negotiate, talk to them, convince them that taking that action will annihilate some of the world's population and have dire consequences for decades to come. Get across to them that this is not an option. It's a lose-lose proposition. We are all human, but we don't need to kill each other because you kicked sand in my face or called me a name. Find ways to communicate and negotiate!!! That's what effective leaders do. They use their human relations skills intermingled with wisdom to lead people to a better life!

Start communicating! Analyze your behavior. It's as simple as me realizing that sometimes I don't talk loudly enough in the classroom for the back row to hear me. I have learned to speak up and adjust to the audience. Can they handle your message? Is it difficult material? Is extra time needed to absorb it? Good communication takes time. Teachers usually ask if there are any questions, wait 2-3 seconds and then continue. Why not wait at least 10 seconds to let students formulate questions they may have?

We are communicating all of the time whether we know it or not. The driver who doesn't use their turn signal is still sending a signal. A signal that either they are lazy, or not focused on their driving. The drunk at the bar may be communicating that he doesn't care or has problems. The employee who is habitually late to work may be communicating that he really doesn't enjoy working there. The student looking elsewhere in the classroom is communicating indifference or unpreparedness. We are all continually communicating whether it be with action or inaction.

Reputation is also part of communication. They call it your "brand" on social media. What is your reputation in the office? Are you the office "Know-it-all," or the office "Flirt?" Acquiring a not so positive reputation can kill your career chances because no one may take you seriously or they may try to avoid you or consider you a bore. If the workplace looks at you as a flake or someone not to be trusted it is VERY difficult to reverse that kind of reputation. It may take years, if you can at all. You may not have a choice and you may have to start over with another company. Instead, be a "go to" person for the right reasons. Be an employee who lives up to your own high standards. If you are honest, dependable and hardworking, people will gravitate towards you and you'll be a leader. Also, when you live up to your own standards, I guarantee you'll exceed company goals and expectations every time!

Research on first impressions tells us that we transmit signals about ourselves when we walk into a room. People size us up in *seven seconds*. "And these computations are made at lightning speed—making major decisions about one another in the first seven seconds of meeting. In business interactions, first impressions are crucial. While you can't stop people from making snap decisions—

the human brain is hardwired in this way as a prehistoric survival mechanism—you *can* understand how to make those decisions work in your favor. First impressions are more heavily influenced by nonverbal cues. In fact, studies have found that nonverbal cues have over four times the impact on the impression you make than anything you say." Here are seven nonverbal ways to make a positive first impression:

1. **Adjust your attitude**. People pick up your attitude instantly. Before you turn to greet someone, or enter the boardroom, or step onstage to make a presentation, think about the situation and make a conscious choice about the attitude you want to embody.
2. **Straighten your posture**. Status and power are nonverbally conveyed by height and space. Standing tall, pulling your shoulders back, and holding your head straight are all signals of confidence and competence.
3. **Smile**. A smile is an invitation, a sign of welcome. It says, "I'm friendly and approachable."
4. **Make eye contact**. Looking at someone's eyes transmits energy and indicates interest and openness. (To improve your eye contact, make a practice of noticing the eye color of everyone you meet.)
5. **Raise your eyebrows**. Open your eyes slightly more than normal to simulate the "eyebrow flash" that is the universal signal of recognition and acknowledgement.
6. **Shake hands**. This is the quickest way to establish rapport. It's also the most effective. Research shows it takes an average of three hours of continuous interaction to develop the same level of rapport that you can get with a

single handshake. (Practice giving a firm, but not vice-like, handshake.)
7. **Lean in slightly**. Leaning forward shows you're engaged and interested. But be respectful of the other person's space. That means, in most business situations, staying about two feet away. (Goman, 2011)

Another view of first impressions says it takes just *three seconds* for someone to determine whether they like you and want to do business with you. Here are four additional assumptions people make about you:

1. **If you're trustworthy**. Princeton researchers found that people decide on your trustworthiness in as little as a tenth of a second. It doesn't take us long to figure out if we can trust someone.
2. **If you're high-status**. A small Dutch study found that people wearing name-brand clothes were seen as higher status and wealthier than folks wearing nondesigner clothes when they approached 80 shoppers in a mall.
3. **If you're smart**. A 2007 study by Nora A. Murphy, a professor at Loyola Marymount University, found that looking your conversation partner in the eye might help encourage people to see you as more intelligent. "Looking while speaking was a key behavior," she wrote. Wearing thick glasses and speaking expressively could help, too.
4. **If you're dominant**. Bald isn't just beautiful, it's powerful. University of Pennsylvania researchers found that it was specifically *shaved* heads that people seemed to associate with dominance— not just the lack of hair. So if it's starting to go,

you might want to shave it. (Baer and Lebowitz, 2015)

Finally, according to Brian Tracy, when you first meet a person, he or she makes a judgment about you in approximately *four seconds*, and judgment is finalized largely within 30 seconds of the initial contact. In a survey of the members of the American Personnel Consultants, those men and women who are responsible for hiring people for large companies generally agreed that they made their decision to hire or not to hire a person within 30 seconds of the first meeting. Retrieved from URL: (https://www.briantracy.com/glob/leadership-success/the-importance-of-a-first-impression)

In summary, whether it's 3, 4, or 7 seconds, we know the power of a positive first impression cannot be overemphasized. Taking a different tack, how long does it take to overcome a bad first impression? Who knows? You might not get a second chance or it may take many, many subsequent positive interactions to overcome that first bad impression. When we first meet someone, we compare every meeting thereafter to that initial one. A positive first impression should set the stage for success!

I was lucky enough to take the *Dale Carnegie* course and I would highly recommend it! At the first session the instructor in the class was very genuine and seemed to care deeply about all of us. He was so smooth that I recoiled slightly wondering what he wanted and I was suspicious of his intentions. It shouldn't be that way and I had no basis for my suspicions. But that's what society does to us. It conditions us to be wary and not reveal much about ourselves, wondering what the other person wants. Scams on television, dishonest salespeople, and spoof phone calls to get personal information all contribute to our healthy skepticism. Some suspicions are well-founded, but most are not. Be genuine in your communications with others. They will reciprocate and you'll make a positive first impression every time!

Communication model

The communication model has four basic elements: *sender, receiver, message*, and *feedback*. More complex models include variables such as: channels, frame of reference, noise, encode/decode, and environment.

We all know that the *sender* is the person who sends the message, but the sender must decide what to send, how to send, and when to send for the receiver to fully comprehend the message. In order for shared meaning to occur the sender needs to "encode" the message in terms the receiver can understand. Oftentimes the message itself (what you're sending) will dictate the channel to be used. For example, if you have to fire someone, you'll do that face-to-face out of respect for the employee. If it's a small policy change, then email will suffice.

When the message has been sent, the *receiver* must interpret that message. The receiver "decodes" the message, hopefully correctly. However, this is where *feedback* plays such an important role. To lower the risk of miscommunication the receiver "feedsback" what they thought the message was about. This gives the receiver the opportunity to ask questions or to clarify. In turn, the sender can then correct, or adjust the message to make sure it's intended meaning is interpreted correctly. Hopefully, through shared meaning, the communication was successful. For example, when you call to make an office appointment the receptionist will repeat the day and time of your appointment before ending the call. This is a double-check so you'll arrive at the right time. It's achieving the goal of effective communication!

Throughout the entire communication process, three things are at play simultaneously: *frame of reference, noise*, and *environment. Frame of reference* is where the person's coming from. It includes age, gender, educational status, and life experience. It's everything that makes us, us. It involves filtering because we filter things through our own experience and frame of reference. So if someone talks about the Vietnam War that will mean something different to me than to a younger person. It's our frame of reference that's different. *Noise*, is anything that interferes with the message. It can be internal or external noise. External noise can be controlled and consists of any noise outside the envelope of the communication, such as: phones ringing, traffic noise, loud music, a baby's cry in church, or even office lighting. We can control all of that type of noise. For instance, if we're standing outside and I'm telling you a joke when a transit bus goes by, I can simply pause and wait for the noise to abate before continuing. On the other hand, internal noise <u>cannot</u> be controlled by the sender; it's the condition of the receiver. That's noise between our ears and the sender has no control over that. Daydreaming, sleepiness, fake listening, or not feeling well, can all be internal noise. If you're physically hurt or not feeling well that can take precedence over actively listening. Our adult attention span is <u>8 seconds</u>, so it's no wonder we miscommunicate. You must find a way to keep the person engaged in the conversation to have a chance at true communication.

The following are Attention Span Statistics:

Statistics	Data
The average attention span in 2015	8.25 seconds
The average attention span in 2000	12 seconds
The average attention span of a goldfish	9 seconds
Percent of teens who forget major details of close friends and relatives	25%
Percent of people who forget their own birthdays from time to time	7%
Average number of times per hour an office worker checks their email inbox	30

Retrieved from URL: (https://www.statisticbrain.com/attention-span-statistics/)

The *environment* encompasses the whole communication model. It surrounds the entire communication process. The time, the place, our culture, physical space, relationships, and even colors influence our communication.

- **Time**. When are you communicating? Is it at a time the receiver can effectively give feedback? Is the communication rushed because of a deadline?
- **Place**. Are you in a noisy atmosphere? Are there distractions? Can the receiver focus on what the sender is meaning?
- **Culture**. Is proper etiquette followed? Are the words appropriate for the person's culture? Are there slang words that can be misinterpreted?
- **Physical space**. Is the boss sitting behind a big oak desk and you're sitting at half that height? How close are you physically when you communicate? (*proxemics*-study of how we use space)
- **Relationships**. Are you equals communicating, or who has the power in the relationship? Are you speaking to an audience or to one person?
- **Colors**. There are colors of receptiveness and colors of avoidance. Generally, red is anger-energy-passion, blue is trust-peace-coldness, yellow is optimistic-cheerful-impatience, and green is balance- growth-possessiveness. Retrieved 12/12/2017 from URL: (www.empower-yourself-with-color-psychology.com)

Why is it so Difficult to Communicate?

Lack of communication is the number one cause of divorce. You must constantly communicate your needs and desires because love can't guess, it doesn't know what you want until you communicate. Many people think communication is easy, it's not! For instance, I tend to interrupt my wife because I think I know what she's going to say (that's the teacher in me), but she takes that as being rude and disrespectful. I'm trying to learn to let her finish talking before I start. It seems so simple, but I didn't realize that I was doing that. When we love someone we assume they know our thoughts and what we want. They don't. We must communicate that to them. Communication is not an innate skill we're born with, we must learn to express ourselves appropriately and at the right time.

We spend a lot of time listening. Adults spend an average of 70% of their time engaged in some sort of communication. Of this, research shows that an average of 45% is spent listening compared to 30% speaking, 16% reading and 9% writing. (Adler, R. et al. 2001). That is, by any standards, a lot of time listening. It is worthwhile taking a bit of extra time to ensure that you listen effectively.

***The biggest communication problem is we do not listen to understand. We listen to reply.

Time Spent Communicating

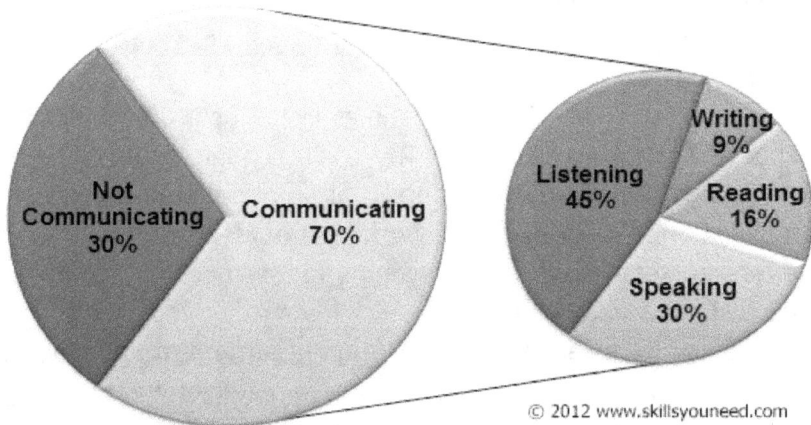

© 2012 www.skillsyouneed.com

Based on the research of: *Adler, R., Rosenfeld, L. and Proctor, R. (2001) Interplay: the process of interpersonal communicating (8th edn), Fort Worth, TX: Harcourt*

Listening is not the same as hearing. Hearing refers to the sounds that enter your ears. It is a physical process that, provided you do not have any hearing problems, happens automatically.
Listening, however, requires more than that: it requires focus and concentrated effort, both mental and sometimes physical as well.

Listening means paying attention not only to the story, but how it is told, the use of language and voice, and how the other person uses his or her body. In other words, it means being aware of both verbal and non-verbal messages. Your ability to listen effectively depends on the degree to which you perceive and understand these messages. It is not a passive process. In fact, the listener can, and should, be at least as engaged in the process as the speaker. The phrase 'active listening' is used to describe this process of being fully involved.

Good listening skills also have benefits in our personal lives, including:
A greater number of friends and social networks, improved self-esteem and confidence, higher grades at school and in academic work and even better health and general well-being.

Studies have shown that, whereas speaking raises blood pressure, attentive listening can bring it down. Retrieved from URL: (https://www.skillsyouneed.com/ips/listening-skills.html)

We can definitely hear without listening. Listening is an acquired skill that must be practiced daily. There is no course on listening that I know of. There are workshops that point out ways to improve listening but we have to work on it ourselves. We know our attention span is only *eight* seconds, so it's imperative that we actively listen to what is being said. For instance, if you tend to "zone out," or fall asleep, during the Sunday sermon then find ways to focus. Try writing down a brief outline to highlight what is being said, or think about how it applies to you. In our stressful society, the stress manifests itself easily through daydreaming. We just have too much on our minds.

My friend related a story about taking a yoga class. He told me that it wasn't beneficial for several weeks because he realized that while he was stretching his body, his mind was still racing. He was thinking about the day's events and what he wanted to accomplish when he returned home, and so forth. Once he discovered that all of those problems and concerns would still be there at the end of the yoga session, and that it did no good to worry about them, he began to realize benefits. He learned to let his mind float free for an hour and relax his body at the same time. Is that why we have trouble sleeping? We can't let go of events of the day and they intrude on our sleep when we should be unwinding. It's hard to stop thinking about the difficult client or the run-in with the boss this afternoon. But compartmentalizing thoughts can help manage our emotions and prioritizing tasks are effective stress management techniques. Be in the moment, focus fully on what you are doing, (it's called "flow" when you're totally immersed in the task at hand) then after you've completed it, move on to the next task.
It is challenging to be an active listener. There are so many things to get done and so much on our minds that we act like we're

listening so we can continue working on our agenda for the day. Effective communication is tough!

Male & Female Communication

We all know that there are many differences in the way males and females communicate. The following is from an article by Richard Drobnick, entitled "5 Ways Men & Women Communicate Differently."

1. **Why talk?**
   He believes communication should have a clear purpose. Behind every conversation is a problem that needs solving or a point that needs to be made. Communication is used to get to the root of the dilemma as efficiently as possible.

   She uses communication to discover how she is feeling and what it is she wants to say. She sees conversation as an act of sharing and an opportunity to increase intimacy with her partner. Through sharing, she releases negative feelings and solidifies her bond with the man she loves.

2. **How Much Should You Say?**
   He prioritizes productivity and efficiency in his daily life, and conversation is no exception. When he tells a story he has already sorted through the muck in his own head, and shares only those details that he deems essential to the point of the story. He might wonder, "Why do women need to talk as much as they do?" Often he will interrupt a woman once he has heard enough to offer a solution.

   She uses communication to explore and organize her thoughts—to discover the point of the story. She may not know what information is necessary or excessive until the words come spilling out. But a woman isn't necessarily searching for a solution when she initiates a conversation. She's looking for someone to listen and understand what she's feeling.

3. **What Does It Mean To Listen?**

   He is conditioned to listen actively. When a woman initiates conversation he assumes she is seeking his advice or assistance. He engages with the woman, filtering everything she's saying through the lens of, "What can we actually do about this?" Learning to listen patiently—not just passively—doesn't come easily for him.

   She sees conversation as a productive end in and of itself. If she feels sufficiently heard or understood she may not need to take further action to resolve a problem or "make things better." The fact that she has been listened to assuages her anxieties and dulls the pangs of negative feelings. Sharing with someone who understands and loves her heals her from the inside and equips her with the emotional tools necessary to handle the trials and tribulations of the outside world.

4. **When *She* Is Feeling Down ...**

   He will want to tackle her problems head on, like a fireman. He feels impatient to put the fire out as quickly as possible. For him, the quickest way to put the fire out is by giving solutions. Because he wants so badly to provide for his spouse, he may take her mood personally and defend himself. He might hear things literally, not realizing that when his spouse is upset she will use words as tools to explore and express difficult emotions.
   By using words as tools to explore and express her difficult emotions when she is upset, she is able to process her negative emotions and let them go. She values support and nurture, and is most fulfilled by sharing, cooperation and community. When he shows interest in her by asking caring questions or expressing heartfelt concerns she

feels loved and cared for. He is fulfilling her first primary love need.

5. **When *He* Is Feeling Down ...**
    He will often withdraw into his "cave" (becoming quiet and withdrawn) when he's upset or stressed. A man's "cave time" is like a short vacation: he reduces stress by forgetting about his problems and focusing on other things like watching television, reading, or playing video games.

    He might avoid communication with his spouse during times of duress. If she persists with nurturing questions or criticism, he withdraws even further, fearing that his partner doesn't trust him to take care of business on his own. However, with her support and understanding, a man will return and be more emotionally available, caring, and loving.

    She might interpret her spouse's silence as a sign that she is failing him or that she's losing him. She instinctively tries to nurture him through his problems by asking an abundance of caring questions. Or she may react defensively out of fear that her own need for healthy open communication is not being respected within the relationship. Ultimately, she can do more for him by appreciating his space, which shows him that she trusts him to work out the problem on his own. Trusting is one of the greatest gifts she has to offer him. In the meantime she should do something nurturing for herself, so she won't resent him when he emerges from his "cave time."

Communication Breaks Down When ...
He feels like he's being told what to do. The most important thing to a man is doing a good job. When his competence is questioned he'll not only feel hurt, but he'll throw up a wall of resistance, and communication begins to breakdown. He thrives in an environment

where he's the expert. Rather than being told, "You should do X" he is likely to respond better to, "What do you think of X?" The trick to improving him is to resist telling him what to do.

She hears from her spouse that her problems aren't as real and pressing as they seem in that very moment. Her spouse may mistakenly think he's being helpful in providing "reality checks" like: "You're making a mountain out of a mole *hill*" or "You're getting overly emotional about it." To her it feels like he is attempting to minimize her feelings or talk her out of having them.

Men and women desire to satisfy their partners, but they may miss the mark because it is truly difficult to understand and accept our partner's different ways of communication. Men and women need education on these differences to help their relationships. Retrieved from URL: (https://psychcentral.com/blog/archives/2012/04/01/6-ways-men-and-women-communicate-differently)

When communicating with the opposite sex, it is worth bearing these differences in mind and trying to work with them rather than against them. For example, as a woman talking to a man, it is worth trying to make your point clear and to the point. If you are making a large and complicated point, break it down into chunks that he can fully understand before moving onto your next point. While women find it easy to follow large statements, a man may find that he is overwhelmed and struggle to remember everything you were saying. Also make sure that you do not interrupt him. Men talking to women should bear in mind that women respond well to your emotional reactions. If she is making what your feel to be a long and complicated point, try to follow it rather than breaking it down for her. Try not to solve her problems for her, but instead try to focus on the emotional aspect of what she is communicating and connect with that instead. These techniques can take a while to master, as unconscious conversation techniques take time and effort to alter, but it is worth bearing in mind that making an effort to speak the other gender's language can make a real difference in your communication with them. Retrieved from URL: (http://www.healthguidance.org/entry/13970/1/Communication-Differences-Between-Men-and-Women)

A woman's communication style is that of feelings and collaboration, whereas men stress communication efficiency and competition. It is important to learn to adjust to the communication preferences of the opposite sex, whether they are your spouse or colleagues at work.

2. Expectations

***High expectations are the key to everything -- Sam Walton

Aren't expectations a drag when they're not met? Isn't it a shame that we don't expect good service anymore? And when we do receive good service, since it's rare, we write the person's name down and remember to do business with them again. Whether it's a restaurant, a work organization, or your spouse we have expectations that shouldn't be ignored.

What do you expect when you go to a restaurant? Other than the building itself, (cleanliness, etc.) you expect:

- A friendly greeting
- An enjoyable atmosphere
- Attentive wait staff to check on you periodically
- Refills when necessary
- Good food
- Accurate tab

The restaurant business is a tough business because expectations are different for each customer. A restaurant is in the service industry which deals with intangibles. Some people want their food and to be left alone, while others want to be waited on hand and foot. If their water or coffee level is down slightly they demand a refill. Therefore, the wait staff must size up each table and try to meet its expectations for good service.

What about work expectations?

- Consistent rules and policies
- Dependable co-workers
- Fair management
- Safe work environment
- Timely training
- Challenging, enjoyable work
- A full day's work for a full day's pay
- Qualified managers and leaders
- Recognition and appreciation

These are simply common workplace expectations. Many expectations are learned when hired, through orientation. They tell us what we can and cannot do in the organization. We are told our job responsibilities so we know our duties for the organization. It's their expectations of us. These are critical if the company is to be efficient and remain competitive in the industry. So the company trains us and we know what to expect, but what about the expectations we have of the boss? We have a right to expect them to be fair, to be good role models, to keep us apprised of company developments, to give us a raise as soon as is practicable, and to make needed training available to keep skills refreshed. Develop the type of relationship where you can talk to your boss about expectations. If you fear reprisal, or they won't listen, then find another job where you can communicate well with management! There are poor bosses out there who are not qualified or are on a power trip and unless the company realizes it and corrects it, things will never change. Hey, you'll be working for 40+ years, find a job where you'll be happy!

<u>What do you expect of coworkers?</u> We spend 30% of our lives at work, so here are things you might expect from coworkers:

- To be dependable
- Not spread gossip
- To do their fair share of work
- To not take credit for others' work
- To be honest
- Always have your back

When coworkers don't meet expectations, it can sour your job. Work with them tactfully so they might learn your expectations and live up to them. And be a good role model yourself!

<u>What about spousal expectations?</u> There are many expectations you have of one another. These include:

- Support (financial and emotional)
- Commitment
- Trust
- Love and respect
- Good communication

You can make your own list of spousal expectations, but if you're not happy at home (with your spouse) and you're not happy at work, then you've got problems. It will be easier to sit with your mate and talk about expectations than it will be with the boss because at home, your equals. If you didn't take time before marriage to discuss expectations, it's never too late. Where love is involved, everything is negotiable. A couple should talk about:

- Who cooks
- Who handles finances
- When/if you want to start a family
- How to handle in-laws

- Who to visit on holidays
- Who maintains the house/yard/cars
- If you plan to buy a house or rent
- What about job relocation?
- Do you both plan to work?

Your expectations, more than anything else in life, determine your reality. When it comes to achieving your goals, if you don't believe you'll succeed, you won't.

***Nobody succeeds beyond his or her wildest expectations unless he or she begins with some wild expectations –
Ralph Charell

Research from LSU shows that people who believe in themselves use more metacognitive functions than those who don't. This means that they use more of their brains and have more brainpower to solve problems. Metacognition is especially important for achievement as it ensures that you approach problems from many different angles and adapt your approach as needed.

The tricky thing about your expectations is that they impact other people too. As far back as the 1960s, Harvard research demonstrated the power of our beliefs in swaying other people's behavior. When teachers in the studies were told that certain (randomly selected) children were smart, those kids performed better, not only in the classroom, but also on standardized IQ tests.

Indeed, we get the most out of other people when we believe in them. Research shows that this happens because when we believe in someone,

- we treat them better than people we think will fail,
- we give them more opportunities to succeed than we give those we think will fail,
- we give them more accurate, helpful feedback than we

give others, and
- we do more teaching because we believe it's time well spent.

Your expectations shape your reality. They can change your life, emotionally and physically. You need to be extra careful about (and aware of) the expectations you harbor as the wrong ones make life unnecessarily difficult. Be especially wary of the expectations that follow—they give people all kinds of trouble.

1. Life should be fair. We've all been told a million times (and likely told other people) that life isn't fair, but in spite of what we know about the intricacies of injustice, it's a concept that doesn't quite sink in in practice. A surprising number of us subconsciously expect life to be fair, and we believe that any unfairness that we experience will somehow be balanced out, even if we don't do anything about it. If you're stuck in that mindset, it's time to get over it (work on your *emotional intelligence* if this is a struggle for you, see Chapter 5). When something "unfair" happens, don't rely on outside forces to get you back on your feet. Sometimes there isn't any consolation prize, and the sooner you stop expecting there to be, the sooner you can take actions that will actually make a difference.

2. Opportunities will fall into my lap. One of the most important things a person can do is stick his or her neck out and seek opportunity. Just because you deserve a raise, a promotion, or a company car, doesn't mean it's going to happen. You have to make it happen. You have to put in the hard work, then go and get what's yours. If we limit ourselves to what's given to us, we are at the mercy of other people. When you take action, think "what steps do I need to take?" "what obstacles are in my way and what do I need to do to remove them?" and "what mistakes am I making that take me away from my goals rather than toward them?"

3. Everyone should like me. People have hang ups, and that means all sorts of decent, kind, respectable people are not liked by (some) others, for no good reason at all. When you think that everyone should like you, you end up with hurt feelings when you shouldn't. (You can't win them all.) When you assume that people are going to like you, you take shortcuts; you start making requests and demands before you've laid the groundwork to really understand what the other person is thinking and feeling. Instead of expecting that people will like you, focus on earning their trust and respect.

4. People should agree with me. This one can be tough. Sure, you know what you're talking about, and for that reason, people should take you seriously, but expecting people to agree with you out of courtesy or because your ideas are so incredibly sound is another story. Something that's obvious to you might not be so to someone with different experiences and a different agenda, so stop being offended when people disagree with you, and stop assuming that there is only one right answer (yours). Instead, focus on how you can find solutions that give everyone what they need.

5. People know what I'm trying to say. People can't read your mind, and what you're trying to say is rarely what other people hear. You can't expect people to understand you just because you're talking—you have to be clear. Whether you're asking someone to do something without providing the context or explaining a complex concept behind a big project, it's easy to leave out relevant information because *you* don't think it's necessary. Communication isn't anything if it isn't clear, and your communication won't be clear until you take the time to understand the other person's perspective.

6. I'm going to fail. If you expect to fail, you stand a higher chance of creating the very outcome you're worried about (self-fulfilling prophecy). If you fail, accept that sometimes you'll fail and sometimes you'll succeed, but if you pursue an endeavor, believe with all your being that you're going to succeed in that endeavor. Otherwise, you'll limit the chances of that happening.

7. Things will make me happy. Sure, things can make life more fun and comfortable in the short run, but they can't make you happy in the long run. Too many of us expect a future event ("I'll be happy when I get that promotion") to make us happy, instead of looking more deeply into the real causes of our unhappiness. If you don't fix what's going on inside, no external event or item is going to make you happy, no matter how much you want it to.

8. I can change him/her. There's only one person in this world you can truly change—yourself—and even that takes a tremendous amount of effort. The only way that people change is through the desire and wherewithal to change themselves. Still, it's tempting to try to change someone who doesn't want to change, as if your sheer will and desire for them to improve will change them (as it has you). You might even actively choose people with problems, thinking that you can "fix" them. Let go of this faulty expectation. Build your life around genuine, positive people, and avoid problematic people that bring you down.

Bringing It All Together. Believing that you'll succeed really does make it more likely that you will. It also means that you'll need to let go of some erroneous expectations that will only get in your way. (Bradberry, 2016) Retrieved from URL: (https://www.forbes.com/sites/travisbradberry/2016/08/02/8-unrealistic-expectations-that-will-ruin-you/2/#6b43fc971dcf)

***Expect more from yourself than from others.

Earl Nightingale, in his video, *The Strangest Secret*, tells us that "we become what we think about most of the time." It's true. If you have high expectations for yourself to succeed, you've planted the seeds to do just that! And chances are if you have high expectations for others, those expectations will be met, also.

Types of Communication (formal, informal)

In an organization, there are two channels of communication: formal and informal. *Formal communication* is pre-defined by the organization. It is also called the "chain of command," because the organization chart shows exactly who reports to whom. The three types of formal communication consist of downward, horizontal, and upward. *Downward communication* contains policies, instructions, and directives in the form of oral or written communication from bosses to subordinates. The message flows downward from upper levels of the company. This type of communication is usually taught in new employee orientation. For example, you must report up each level of the organization. You cannot jump formal levels and write the CEO an email or you'll be reprimanded. We are told everything flows through our immediate supervisor. It's certainly nothing personal. It simply makes communication more efficient and organized. *Horizontal communication* is communication between individuals at the same level in the organization. For example, first line supervisors may have meetings periodically to coordinate production goals, or to simply decide on how to handle various problems that may arise. *Upward communication* should be the easiest, but sometimes it's the most difficult to achieve of the three types of formal communication. Why? Because management may feel that asking for or receiving input from subordinates is too time-consuming so they decide matters themselves. Do you feel comfortable offering suggestions to your boss? Most of us don't. In the modern trend of "teamwork," we should be able to talk to the boss about most things without fear of repercussion. However, it can be risky. When you've been on the job for two days and an upper-level manager asks how you like it so far, you're not going to say, "Man, this job sucks." There is no need to be brutally honest, just simply say that it's going to be challenging work. If your boss holds grudges or subscribes to "authoritarian-style management," chances are he or she will not be prone to listen. Another caution:

if the employee suggestion box is located directly over the paper shredder, you're probably not being heard!

Informal communication can be defined as the grapevine. Every organization has one and there are no formal lines of communication because it deals with gossip. We are social beings and we like casual talk and thoughts of others. Through casual conversation at lunch we discuss the boss and what's going on in the office. Research reveals that if the organization is healthy, the grapevine should carry only gossip. For example, "did you hear that..." or "I wonder why he stays late every time she does." Many people buy into the office gossip. But when the grapevine carries messages such as: "I heard Joe was laid off, he didn't quit" or "a person in the other department heard that management is considering shutting down our department," it affects morale. It is an indicator that upper levels in the organization are not communicating properly with their employees.

Though the grapevine is prone to carry negative information, it is also prone to be accurate. Rather than being a source of unfounded gossip, the grapevine has an accuracy of 75% to 95% (Caudron, 1998; Walton, 1961, pp. 45-49). Of course, some entirely false rumors are also spread through the grapevine, especially the electronic grapevine (Pitts, 1999). However, grapevine information can be confirmed while rumors cannot. Grapevine messages are often more accurate than formal ones because status, power, and rank differences seem less important. In one study, middle managers reported that they often found informal communication to be a better source of organizational information than formal communication (Harcourt, Richerson, & Waitterk, 1991). Isn't that sad?

BASIS FOR COMPARISON	FORMAL COMMUNICATION	INFORMAL COMMUNICATION
Meaning	A type of verbal communication in which the interchange of information is done through the pre-defined channels is known as formal communication.	A type of verbal communication in which the interchange of information does not follow any channels i.e. the communication stretches in all directions.
Another Name	Official Communication	Grapevine communication
Reliability	More	Comparatively less
Speed	Slow	Very Fast
Evidence	As the communication is generally written, documentary evidence is present.	No documentary evidence.
Time Consuming	Yes	No
Advantage	Effective due to timely and	Efficient because employees can

BASIS FOR COMPARISON	FORMAL COMMUNICATION	INFORMAL COMMUNICATION
	systematic flow of information.	discuss work related problems, this saves time and cost of the organization.
Disadvantage	Distortion due to long chain of communication.	Spread of rumors
Secrecy	Full secrecy is maintained.	It is difficult to maintain the secrecy.
Flow of Information	Only through predefined channels.	Can move freely.

Retrieved from URL: (https://keydifferences.com/difference-between-formal-and-informal-communication.html)

Nonverbal communication is massive in meaning. Nonverbal and verbal must be in sync for true communication to take place. If they are not synchronized, people always take nonverbal over what you are saying (verbal) when interpreting the message. The old cliché, "It's not what you say, it's how you say it," is true. When you're communicating, people take into account everything: eye contact, facial expression, body posture, leg and arm movement, and head movement. If your body betrays your message you might also appear untrustworthy. Watching people's body language is fun to play with and we learn to mask nonverbal as we age, but children do not hide it--if they're unhappy or mad then it's crossed legs, crossed arms and possibly no eye contact. They are letting you know their feelings in no uncertain terms.

What Effective Communication will do for You

Effective communication is critical to any organization and can help it in many ways. In fact, communication plays a role in product development, customer relations, employee management – virtually every facet of a business' operations. Employees are a key audience because they often serve as the conduit to other audiences. If employees are informed and engaged, communications with other constituencies are likely to be strong as well (Richards).
Retrieved from URL: (http://smallbusiness.chron.com/effective-communication-organization-1400.html)

Effective communication is an important life skill that enables us to better understand and connect with the people around us. It allows us to build respect and trust, resolve differences and foster environments where problem solving, caring, affection and creative ideas can thrive. Lack of effective communication inadvertently leads to conflict and frustration in both professional and personal relationships. Retrieved from URL: (https://www.reference.com/business-finance/importance-effective-communication-a4a765768f3ac4#)

Finally, effective communication may get you all of the following: a spouse, a raise, a better deal on a car, help you understand mortgage terms, clarify, make life easier, get you a promotion, viewed as a leader, a team member who can be counted on, liked by subordinates, liked by colleagues, respect in your field/career, a reputation as a truthful/clear communicator, or asked to give presentations. Yes, everything in our lives involves communication, but make it effective communication!

***No matter what job you have in life, your success will be determined 5% by your academic credentials, 15% by your professional experiences, and 80% by your communication skills.

IN-YOUR-FACE CHALLENGE

Now that you've read the chapter you have no more excuses to miscommunicate! So get off your ass, stop mumbling, and start sending clear messages! Let your expectations be known and expect the best from others. Chances are, they won't let you down. I wish you success!

References

Baer, D. & Lebowitz, S. (2015, November 18). Science says people decide these 13 things within seconds of meeting you. *Business Insider*. (http://www.businessinsider.com/science-of-first-impressions-2015-11/)
Caudron, S. (1998). They hear it through the grapevine. *Workforce*, 77(11), 25-27.

Goman, C.K. (2011, February 13). Seven Seconds to Make a First Impression. (https://www.forbes.com/sites/carolkinseygoman/2011/02/13seven-seconds-to-make-a-first-impression)

Harcourt, J., Richerson, V., & Waitterk, M.J. (1991). A national study of middle managers' assessment of organization communication quality. *Journal of Business Communication*, 28, 348-365.

Pitts, L., Jr. (1999, January 20). Rumors yield sour fruit on electronic grapevine. *Fort Worth Star-Telegram*, p. 13.

Surbhi, S. (2015, March 27). Difference Between Formal and Informal Communication. (https://keydifferences.com/difference-between-formal-and-informal-communication.html)

Walton, E. (1961). How effective is the grapevine? *Personnel*, 28, 46.

Chapter Two – Values & Ethics

Almost every college textbook includes a chapter on values and ethics. Why? It is important that we uphold certain values and know how to treat people fairly in any relationship, be it business or personal. We're losing sight of our values due to greed and loss of conscience in business. Golden Rule management says that we should treat other people the way we'd like to be treated. The Golden Rule has been around a long time, that's why it's Golden! It is generally believed that we develop basic values by approximately seven years of age, so let's explore values.

1. Values

***Values are like fingerprints. Nobody's are the same, but you leave them all over everything you do. -- Elvis Presley

How did we develop our First Values and Beliefs?

When we were kids, the values and beliefs our parents and families talked about and acted on became a large part of our first value system. Our friends and peer groups were the next major influence. We learned from them about values that were different from our family's beliefs. The beliefs and behaviors of our heroes and people we admired also left a mark on our developing values. Formal institutions like school, media, and organized religion also instilled values within us. Societal values demonstrated through the laws and courts had some influence on developing our value systems. A lot of people helped you form your values and beliefs. Retrieved from URL: (http://www.usdrugrehabcenters.com/the-relapse-prevention-plan/chapter-nine/how-did-we-develop-our-first-values-and-beliefs/)

How would you define Your Values?

Before you answer this question, you need to know what, in general, values are.
Your values are the things that you believe are important in the way you live and work.
They (should) determine your priorities, and, deep down, they're probably the measures you use to tell if your life is turning out the way you want it to.

When the things that you do and the way you behave match your values, life is usually good – you're satisfied and content. But when these don't align with your personal values, that's when things feel... wrong. This can be a real source of unhappiness. This is why making a conscious effort to identify your values is so important.

How Values Help You

Values exist, whether you recognize them or not. Life can be much easier when you acknowledge your values – and when you make plans and decisions that honor them.
If you value family, but you have to work 70-hour weeks in your job, will you feel internal stress and conflict? And if you don't value competition, and you work in a highly competitive sales environment, are you likely to be satisfied in your job?

In these types of situations, understanding your values can really help. When you know your own values, you can use them to make decisions about how to live your life, and you can answer questions like these:

- What job should I pursue?
- Should I accept this promotion?
- Should I start my own business?
- Should I compromise, or be firm with my position?
- Should I follow tradition, or travel down a new path?

So, take the time to understand the real priorities in your life, and you'll be able to determine the best direction for you and your <u>life goals</u>!

Tip:

Values are usually fairly stable, yet they don't have strict limits or boundaries. Also, as you move through life, your values may change. For example, when you start your career, success – measured by money and status – might be a top priority. But after you have a family, work-life balance may be what you value more.

As your definition of success changes, so do your personal values. This is why keeping in touch with your values is a lifelong exercise. You should continuously revisit this, especially if you start to feel unbalanced... and you can't quite figure out why.

As you go through the exercise below, bear in mind that values that were important in the past may not be relevant now.

<u>Defining Your Values</u>

When you define your personal values, you discover what's truly important to you. A good way of starting to do this is to look back on your life – to identify when you felt really good, and really confident that you were making good choices.

Step 1: Identify the times when you were happiest

Find examples from both your career and personal life. This will ensure some balance in your answers.
- What were you doing?
- Were you with other people? Who?
- What other factors contributed to your happiness?

Step 2: Identify the times when you were most proud

- Use examples from your career and personal life.
- Why were you proud?
- Did other people share your pride? Who?
- What other factors contributed to your feelings of pride?

Step 3: Identify the times when you were most fulfilled and satisfied

Again, use both work and personal examples.

- What need or desire was fulfilled?
- How and why did the experience give your life meaning?
- What other factors contributed to your feelings of fulfillment?

Step 4: Determine your top values, based on your experiences of happiness, pride, and fulfillment

Why is each experience truly important and memorable? Use the following list of common personal values to help you get started – and aim for about 10 top values. (As you work through, you may find that some of these naturally combine. For instance, if you value philanthropy, community, and generosity, you might say that service to others is one of your top values.)

Accountability	Excellence	Perfection
Accuracy	Excitement	Piety
Achievement	Expertise	Positivity
Adventurousness	Exploration	Practicality
Altruism	Expressiveness	Preparedness
Ambition	Fairness	Professionalism
Assertiveness	Faith	Prudence
Balance	Family-orientedness	Quality-oriented
Being the best	Fidelity	Reliability
Belonging	Fitness	Resourcefulness
Boldness	Fluency	Restraint

Calmness
Carefulness
Challenge
Cheerfulness
Clear-mindedness
Commitment
Community
Compassion
Competitiveness
Consistency
Contentment
Continue to improve
Contribution
Control
Cooperation
Correctness
Courtesy
Creativity
Curiosity
Decisiveness
Democraticness
Dependability
Determination
Devoutness
Diligence
Discipline
Discretion
Diversity
Dynamism
Economy
Effectiveness
Efficiency
Elegance
Empathy
Enjoyment
Enthusiasm

Focus
Freedom
Fun
Generosity
Goodness
Grace
Growth
Happiness
Hard Work
Health
Helping society
Holiness
Honesty
Honor
Humility
Independence
Ingenuity
Inner harmony
Inquisitiveness
Insightfulness
Intelligence
Intellectual status
Intuition
Joy
Justice
Leadership
Legacy
Love
Loyalty
Making a difference
Mastery
Merit
Obedience
Openness
Order
Originality

Results-oriented
Rigor
Security
Self-actualization
Self-control
Selflessness
Self-reliance
Sensitivity
Serenity
Service
Shrewdness
Simplicity
Soundness
Speed
Spontaneity
Stability
Strategic
Strength
Structure
Success
Support
Teamwork
Temperance
Thankfulness
Thoroughness
Thoughtfulness
Timeliness
Tolerance
Traditionalism
Trustworthiness
Truth-seeking
Understanding
Uniqueness
Unity
Usefulness
Vision

Equality   Patriotism   Vitality

Step 5: Prioritize your top values

This step is probably the most difficult, because you'll have to look deep inside yourself. It's also the most important step, because, when making a decision, you'll have to choose between solutions that may satisfy different values. This is when you must know which value is more important to you.

Write down your top values, not in any particular order. Look at the first two values and ask yourself, "If I could satisfy only one of these, which would I choose?" It might help to visualize a situation in which you would have to make that choice. For example, if you compare the values of service and stability, imagine that you must decide whether to sell your house and move to another country to do valuable foreign aid work, or keep your house and volunteer to do charity work closer to home.
Keep working through the list, by comparing each value with each other value, until your list is in the correct order. Since it's so important to identify and prioritize your values, investing your time in this step is definitely worth it.

Step 6: Reaffirm your values

Check your top-priority values, and make sure they fit with your life and your vision for yourself.

- Do these values make you feel good about yourself?
- Are you proud of your top three values?
- Would you be comfortable and proud to tell your values to people you respect and admire?
- Do these values represent things you would support, even if your choice isn't popular, and it puts you in the minority?

When you consider your values in decision making, you can be sure to keep your sense of integrity and what you know is right, and approach decisions with confidence and clarity. You'll also know that what you're doing is best for your current and future happiness and satisfaction. Making value-based choices may not always be easy. However, making a choice that you know is right is a lot less difficult in the long run.

Key Points

Identifying and understanding your values is a challenging and important exercise. Your personal values are a central part of who you are – and who you want to be. By becoming more aware of these important factors in your life, you can use them as a guide to make the best choice in any situation. Some of life's decisions are really about determining what you value most. When many options seem reasonable, it's helpful and comforting to rely on your values – and use them as a strong guiding force to point you in the right direction. Retrieved from URL:
(https://www.mindtools.com/pages/article/newTED_85.htm)

What happens when your values start drifting? When you see others cheating to get ahead or playing politics to get the promotion, do you consider doing the same thing? That is when you need to take stock of your values and priorities. It is difficult to take the long road while people around you are taking short cuts to advance themselves. But it stresses even more the importance of living up to your character, your reputation, and your values. Taking the right path, even if it's longer, will get you to your goal honestly. And you can hold your head up high!

I was in a five mile race that had a red line put down for the runners to follow. It was a cross country course and the line went around a tree on the corner of the course. While I was following the red line around the tree, another runner cut inside the tree to pass me. It saved a few steps but the runner didn't run the full five miles. Do they do it to win a trophy at all costs? Do they not care or have a conscience? Heck, if it's that important then go buy a trophy after the race so you can brag to friends and family. I, myself, can sleep with a clear conscience knowing I ran five miles, not 4.999. As you examine your core values try not to ever let your values drift, regardless of what your coworkers or friends are doing. Always continue building your character. You must answer to yourself and if your conscience is clear then your value system is intact. The rewards will be there for you in the end.

In summary, as we discussed in the previous chapter about Communication being the basis for everything, we can add an important cornerstone to that foundation, and it is Values. When you discover what you value it will help you determine the kind of person you are, what your career should be, how you view society, and even the type of person to marry.

***It's not hard to make decisions once you know what your values are. -- Roy Disney

<u>Positive Attitudes</u>

Values, attitudes, and behavior closely correlate with one another. Envision three building blocks with "values" being the bottom block. As mentioned before, it is the foundation upon which everything else is built. Next, the second building block that rests on the "values" block, is "attitudes." The third, or top, building block would be "behavior." These all work together to form your personality and character.

Behavior
Attitudes
V A L U E S

An **attitude** is a mental position one possesses with regard to a fact, issue, or belief. It is defined as *a general and enduring positive or negative feeling about some person, object, or issue* (Petty & Cacioppo, 1981). It is an emotional readiness to behave in a particular manner. Generally, employees who possess positive attitudes and are open-minded about controversial issues are judged to have more desirable personalities than those with negative attitudes who hold biased and prejudiced viewpoints (Wray et al. 1996, 23).

To see how our values are aligned with our attitudes, think about your attitude towards the following:

- Politics
- Religion
- Cheaters
- Education
- Work
- Charity
- The Homeless
- Parenting
- Children
- Procrastination
- Your neighbors
- Failure

You can't separate values from your attitudes. For example, what is your attitude towards education? Do you believe everyone needs a college degree? Is education a worthwhile investment? Can you make it in the world with only a high school diploma? What about the workplace. Do you believe in working hard for your pay, or taking shortcuts when possible? These are all questions that relate to our value system.

Morale in the Workplace

Sometimes, the kindest thing to do is to tell employees the harsh truth – even if they don't want to hear it. A chat, or an email, a day will keep the resignations away – it's a new take on an old adage but is increasingly important advice for HR professionals struggling with retention.
"Managers can be doing everything right, but if they're not including employees in the information loop, staff engagement could suffer," Accountemps chairman and author of *Human Resources Kit For Dummies*®, 3rd Edition, Max Messmer, said in a statement." To improve communication, keep team members apprised of company goals and performance, and encourage them to ask questions and offer feedback."

The results of a recent study conducted by Accountemps show that 33% of respondents believe inadequate communication from management is the primary cause of morale issues in the workplace. Additionally, the results reveal 18% saw micromanagement as the biggest problem, while 38% thought effective communication was the best possible solution.

In order to decrease the possibility of employee turnover, managers should ensure that they are living up to their roles by serving as good communicators. Whether it's in a group meeting, or on a one-on-one basis with individual workers, employee morale will increase significantly if their immediate superiors are as upfront with them as possible.

With that being said, nearly one-fifth of the survey respondents pointed to micromanagement as a major concern. While it is important for managers to ensure that tasks are being performed properly and in a timely fashion, over-managing the employees adds a level of hostility to the workplace that would be counterproductive to project completion.
However, if there are communication issues in the office, resolving these issues is relatively simple Messmer said. "Fortunately, morale

problems can often be addressed relatively easily. Improving workplace communication is one of the most effective – and one of the least costly – ways to combat the problem of a disengaged workforce," he said.

Here are Accountemps five characteristics of low morale and the remedies:

1. An active grapevine. Failure to communicate leads to gossip and misinformation flourishing in the workplace. Honesty is always the best policy regardless if you have bad news to share or you yourself do not know exact details. By supplying reliable accurate information the more you shut down the rumor mill.

2. Lack of initiative. Unmotivated employees are not proactive, therefore foster an ownership environment in which employees are challenged to take initiative and solve problems in creative ways.

3. Scarce rewards. Step up efforts to recognize employees' efforts with praise, low-cost awards and spot bonuses.

4. Changes in attitude. When employees are unhappy, it shows. Watch out for red flags such as negativity, higher rates of absenteeism, or reduced commitment. Checking in with workers on a regular basis can help gauge morale and address budding problems.

5. Poor performance. Low morale problems can affect work quality. Signs of trouble include missed deadlines, an increase in mistakes or a decline in service levels. Consider bringing in temporary professionals to ease the workload (Hopkins, I., 2013, October 13). Retrieved from URL: (https://www.hcamag.com/hr-news/low-employee-morale-linked-to-lack-of-communication-180904.aspx)

Low employee morale can be a serious concern for a business. Unhappy employees can lead to reduced productivity, poor customer service and problems with employee retention. While incentives such as raises, benefits and employee recognition programs can help increase employee morale, if your company is suffering from low morale, it is vital to be able to identify the root causes.

The first root cause is **Changing Goals**. Constantly changing employee goals can exhaust employees who are trying to do a good job. Being told that something is an important goal is a motivator for good workers, but when they put all their energy and time into accomplishing that goal only to have it discarded for a new goal, the result can be discouragement and a feeling of lack of accomplishment. Employees should be assigned tasks that are possible for them to accomplish, along with clear guidelines about how to accomplish the tasks and clear indicator of when the tasks' goals are accomplished.

The second root cause can be **Misunderstood Expectations**. Nothing brings down morale like confusion. Employees lacking clear guidance can spend days, weeks, or even months on the job not knowing exactly what is expected of them. When this happens they tend to perform poorly by management's standards and often experience a drop in morale as they begin to believe they are wasting their time and the company's. This problem is easily remedied. When a new employee is hired or a new responsibility is assigned to an existing employee, the hiring manager should make the job expectations clear and arrange for proper training on correct procedures and deadlines. An employee who understands the usefulness and methods of completing his tasks each day will have far higher morale than one who wanders aimlessly or spends time doing things that turn out to be unproductive.

The third root cause is **No Open Communication** (there's communication again!). Creating a workplace in which an open line of communication to management is not available is dangerous to staff morale. Employees often have insight into ways to improve workplace procedures or the company's end product, or may have legitimate issues with problematic procedures or staff. If employees don't feel comfortable approaching a boss, either with ideas or problems, management runs the risk of missing out on creative ideas and having problems fester. Employees should be encouraged to voice their ideas and concerns to management without repercussions. Set up guidelines that let employees know how to privately discuss issues, and never make them feel as though they are doing something wrong by doing so.

The final root cause is **Wasted Potential**. Low morale often results from simply wasting talent. People are often hired for jobs that they are overqualified for or who have a different skill set or interests than what the job requires. When this happens, employees can easily get frustrated or bored with the work, and can end up being more concerned about how to leave the company than how to do a good job. Not only is the resulting lack of productivity and potential turnover bad for business, but it robs a person of the ability to reach her true potential. Finding a more appropriate position for an employee may save both the employee and the company frustration and potential financial loss (Morgan/accessed 12/23/2017). Retrieved from URL: (http://smallbusiness.chron.com/causes-low-employee-morale-43267.html)

So what can we do if we work in a "low-morale" organization? Management doesn't seem to care and hasn't tried to correct low-morale, or may not know how. You've tried to communicate concerns to them, but to no avail. Assuming you want to continue working there, you must take charge of your *own attitudes*. Adjust your perceptions as best you can, without compromising your values. Find small victories in doing your job correctly. It shouldn't have to happen but you may need to look outside the company at achieving personal goals to keep your morale from descending into bitterness.

Here are 5 Simple Things That Can Help Change Your Attitude:

- Identify and understand what you want to change. ...

- Look for a role model. ...
- Think about how your attitude change will affect your life. ...
- Choose the right company. ...
- Believe that you are able to change.

Retrieved from URL: (www.lifehack.org/articles/communication/5-tips-how-change-your-attitude-for-the-better)

Positive Attitudes at Work

A positive attitude in the workplace helps employees to accomplish tasks faster and in a better manner. The performance of employees to a great extent depends on the good relationship they share with their colleagues. A good relationship can be established only when employees demonstrate a positive attitude towards their work and colleagues. Through positive energy, work becomes a pleasure and employees find it easier to achieve their goals.

A positive attitude has significant benefits for an individual in many aspects. Let's look at some of them below.

1. Career success: Employees' success in the workplace is measured through their performance. Employees with a positive attitude will always think of ways of accomplishing their task in a well-defined manner instead of complaining or finding excuses for non-performance. This results in success either through promotion or increased compensation.

2. Productivity: With a positive attitude, employees tend to take more interest in what they do and deliver. Consequently, they produce better quality work with minimum errors. This improves their overall output as well as productivity.

3. Leadership: Working in an organization is all about managing a diverse workforce. Some employees earn respect easily and people often follow and listen to them. This is possible through the positive attitude demonstrated by leaders.

4. Team work: Good relationships among employees help them to build effective teams where all the members are united and work for a common cause. A positive attitude helps employees to appreciate each other's competencies and work as a team for achieving common objectives instead of being overly perturbed by inadequacies of team members.

5. Decision making: Having a positive attitude helps employees to make better decisions, in an objective manner. It triggers a healthy thought process, enabling employees to choose wisely and logically.

6. Motivation: Having a positive attitude helps in motivating employees to overcome obstacles that they may face during the course of their job. It also determines the way they see the world around them. The moment they are successful in overcoming obstacles, they are motivated to move forward.

7. Interpersonal relations: Customers prefer to deal with someone who is positive in nature. A positive attitude enables employees to share a better rapport with customers, earning valuable customer loyalty.

8. Stress management: Stress has a detrimental effect on the health of employees. So how can employees cope with it? Stress can be reduced through positive thinking; and with reduced stress, employees will enjoy better health and take fewer sick leaves.

In conclusion, a positive attitude at work is beneficial not only to the organization, but also to the employees on an individual basis (Nag, 2012). Retrieved from URL: (https://blog.commlabindia.com/elearning-design/positive-attitude-at-workplace)

Benefits of Positive Attitudes

Understanding positive thinking and self-talk
Positive thinking doesn't mean that you keep your head in the sand and ignore life's less pleasant situations. Positive thinking just means that you approach unpleasantness in a more positive and productive way. You think the best is going to happen, not the worst.
Positive thinking often starts with self-talk. Self-talk is the endless stream of unspoken thoughts that run through your head. These

automatic thoughts can be positive or negative. Some of your self-talk comes from logic and reason. Other self-talk may arise from misconceptions that you create because of lack of information.

If the thoughts that run through your head are mostly negative, your outlook on life is more likely pessimistic. If your thoughts are mostly positive, you're likely an optimist — someone who practices positive thinking.

The Health Benefits of Positive Thinking

Researchers continue to explore the effects of positive thinking and optimism on health. Health benefits that positive thinking may provide include:

- Increased life span
- Lower rates of depression
- Lower levels of distress
- Greater resistance to the common cold
- Better psychological and physical well-being
- Better cardiovascular health and reduced risk of death from cardiovascular disease
- Better coping skills during hardships and times of stress

It's unclear why people who engage in positive thinking experience these health benefits. One theory is that having a positive outlook enables you to cope better with stressful situations, which reduces the harmful health effects of stress on your body.

It's also thought that positive and optimistic people tend to live healthier lifestyles — they get more physical activity, follow a healthier diet, and don't smoke or drink alcohol in excess.

Focusing on positive thinking
You can learn to turn negative thinking into positive thinking. The process is simple, but it does take time and practice — you're

creating a new habit, after all. Here are some ways to think and behave in a more positive and optimistic way:

Identify areas to change. If you want to become more optimistic and engage in more positive thinking, first identify areas of your life that you usually think negatively about, whether it's work, your daily commute or a relationship. You can start small by focusing on one area to approach in a more positive way.

Check yourself. Periodically during the day, stop and evaluate what you're thinking. If you find that your thoughts are mainly negative, try to find a way to put a positive spin on them.

Be open to humor. Give yourself permission to smile or laugh, especially during difficult times. Seek humor in everyday happenings. When you can laugh at life, you feel less stressed.

Follow a healthy lifestyle. Aim to exercise for about 30 minutes on most days of the week. You can also break it up into 10-minute chunks of time during the day. Exercise can positively affect mood and reduce stress. Follow a healthy diet to fuel your mind and body. And learn techniques to manage stress.

Surround yourself with positive people. Make sure those in your life are positive, supportive people you can depend on to give helpful advice and feedback. Negative people may increase your stress level and make you doubt your ability to manage stress in healthy ways.

Practice positive self-talk. Start by following one simple rule: Don't say anything to yourself that you wouldn't say to anyone else. Be gentle and encouraging with yourself. If a negative thought enters your mind, evaluate it rationally and respond with affirmations of what is good about you. Think about things you're thankful for in your life.

Here are some examples of negative self-talk and how you can apply a positive thinking twist to them:

Putting positive thinking into practice

Negative self-talk	Positive thinking
I've never done it before.	It's an opportunity to learn something new.
It's too complicated.	I'll tackle it from a different angle.
I don't have the resources.	Necessity is the mother of invention.
I'm too lazy to get this done.	I wasn't able to fit it into my schedule, but I can re-examine some priorities.
There's no way it will work.	I can try to make it work.
It's too radical a change.	Let's take a chance.
No one bothers to communicate with me.	I'll see if I can open the channels of communication.
I'm not going to get any better at this.	I'll give it another try.

Practicing positive thinking every day

If you tend to have a negative outlook, don't expect to become an optimist overnight. But with practice, eventually your self-talk will contain less self-criticism and more self-acceptance. You may also become less critical of the world around you.

When your state of mind is generally optimistic, you're better able to handle everyday stress in a more constructive way. That ability may contribute to the widely observed health benefits of positive thinking (Mayo Clinic Staff/accessed 12/23/17). Retrieved from URL: (https://www.mayoclinic.org/healthy-lifestyle/stress-management/in-depth/positive-thinking/art-20043950?pg=1)

Behaviors

Behavior is simply how you conduct yourself in a situation. Our parents told us to be on our "best behavior," in church. Usually meaning not to act up, be quiet, and listen attentively. Behavior is at the top of our three building blocks, with Attitudes in the middle, and Values being the foundation.

How do you behave...

> in a meeting?
> at work?
> while waiting in line?
> in a competitive situation?
> under pressure?
> in an emergency?

Your behavior in various situations will dictate your success at work and in life. We are judged by our behavior and bad behavior could cost you a relationship or a job.

Every employer's dream would most likely be to have employees with glowing behaviors, making management of employees an easy task. With so many issues in the workplace, employers breathe a sigh of relief when they receive the gift of an employee not laden with issues and constantly on the brink of – if not fully – causing problems within the office, or at least at their own desk.

- **Positive 'can-do' attitude**. Being ready, available and willing to get the job done, and done well, should be traits that employees keep on the front burner.
- **Courteous and friendly**. Employees who do their best to be courteous and friendly to their coworkers, managers, and customers make office life much more pleasant than those who seek to cause disturbances or drama. These employees brighten the office and leave their egos and outside problems at the door in the name of being good workers and trying to maintain a good work atmosphere. While no one is perfect and everyone has bad days, these employees manage to rise above the fray.
- **Meet deadlines**. Employees who meet deadlines will also likely be well organized and responsible.
- **Takes responsibility**. While confessing an error can strike fear in the hearts of employees, those who value their work, their word and their future with the company will take responsibility and tell the truth.
- **Good attendance and punctuality**. Being at the job and arriving on time builds trust that you will be there each day. Employers know about employees who frequently arrive late with a variety of excuses, possibly missing early morning meetings, so a punctual and available employee provides the employer peace of mind (Cooper).

Retrieved from URL: (http://smallbusiness.chron.com/examples-good-employee-behavior-13805.html)

2. Ethics

***Ethics are more important than laws. -- Wynton Marsalis

Ethics is a term defined by society. It is knowing right from wrong, but think back in history and look at how ethical attitudes change with societal norms. Do you remember when early television sitcoms wouldn't ever allow a married couple to be shown in the same bed? They slept in twin beds with distance between them. In our 21st century, television now shows unwed couples in the same bed without giving it a second thought. What about language? Nowadays, foul language is acceptable on television, whereas in the past, the censors would never accept such words. Boy, have times changed! Have they changed for the better? Judge for yourself.

Corporations have no ethics because corporate ethics is a reflection of individual ethics within the organization. Individual ethics determine everything a business does. Codes of ethics set forth principles for the organization to live by and should be covered in orientation training of new employees. It simply sets boundaries so employees know, for instance, that they can't accept gifts from their clients for fear of compromising the business relationship.

Individual Ethics

Ethics are learned and developed from the time of birth and continue developing throughout our lifetime. There are theories of how we develop ethics and I agree with Kohlberg's Stages of Moral Development.

Level 1 - Pre-conventional morality
At the pre-conventional level (most nine-year-olds and younger, some over nine), we don't have a personal code of morality. Instead, our moral code is shaped by the standards of adults and the consequences of following or breaking their rules.

Authority is outside the individual and reasoning is based on the physical consequences of actions.

• *Stage 1. Obedience and Punishment Orientation.* The child/individual is good in order to avoid being punished. If a person is punished, they must have done wrong.
• *Stage 2. Individualism and Exchange.* At this stage, children recognize that there is not just one right view that is handed down by the authorities. Different individuals have different viewpoints.

Level 2 - Conventional morality

At the conventional level (most adolescents and adults), we begin to internalize the moral standards of valued adult role models.

Authority is internalized but not questioned, and reasoning is based on the norms of the group to which the person belongs.

• *Stage 3. Good Interpersonal Relationships*. The child/individual is good in order to be seen as being a good person by others. Therefore, answers relate to the approval of others.
• *Stage 4. Maintaining the Social Order*. The child/individual becomes aware of the wider rules of society, so judgments concern obeying the rules in order to uphold the law and to avoid guilt.

Level 3 - Post-conventional morality

Individual judgment is based on self-chosen principles, and moral reasoning is based on individual rights and justice. According to Kohlberg this level of moral reasoning is as far as most people get.

Only 10-15% are capable of the kind of abstract thinking necessary for stage 5 or 6 (post-conventional morality). That is to say, most people take their moral views from those around them and only a minority think through ethical principles for themselves.

• *Stage 5. Social Contract and Individual Rights*. The child/individual becomes aware that while rules/laws might exist for the good of the greatest number, there are times when they will work against the interest of particular individuals
Stage 6. Universal Principles. People at this stage have developed their own set of moral guidelines which may or may not fit the law. The principles apply to everyone (McLeod, 2013).
Retrieved from URL:
(https://www.simplypsychology.org/kohlberg.html)

Kohlberg's theory is easy to understand because it relates roughly to the three stages of life: childhood, teen, and adulthood. When you're a child (pre-conventional) you are concerned about yourself and if you will get punished for your actions if caught. It's all about <u>you</u>! As you reach your teen years (conventional) you start realizing how your decisions affect others and you begin looking outside yourself. When you progress to the adulthood stage (post-conventional) you are a fully functioning good citizen who enhances your community and helps your fellow human beings.

***A man without ethics is a wild beast loosed upon this world.
-- Albert Camus

<u>Ethics in the Workplace</u>

Each failure to practice value-based workplace ethics affects your self-image and what you stand for far more than it affects your coworkers. But the effect of your behavior on your fellow employees is real, tangible, and unpredictable, too.

Following are examples of employees failing to practice fundamental workplace ethics. The solution? Change the behavior, of course. You may never have thought of these actions as problems with ethical behavior - but they are. And, all of them affect your coworkers in negative ways.

What are signs that you know that your actions are substandard? You make up excuses, give yourself reasons, and that little voice of your conscience that chatters away in your head, tries to convince your ethical self that your lapse in workplace ethics is okay.

Here are sixteen examples of employees failing to practice fundamental workplace ethics.

- You are using the company restroom and use up the last roll of toilet paper, or the last piece of paper towel. Without thought for the needs of the next employee, you go back to work rather than addressing the issue.

- You call in sick to your supervisor because it's a beautiful day and you decide to go to the beach, or shopping.
- You engage in an affair with a coworker while married because no one at work will ever know, you think you're in love, you think you can get away with it, your personal matters are your own business, the affair will not impact other employees or the workplace.
- You place your dirty cup in the lunchroom sink. With a guilty glance around the room, you find no one watching and quickly leave the lunchroom.
- Your company sponsors events, activities, or lunches and you sign up to attend and fail to show. Conversely, you fail to sign up and show up anyway. You make the behavior worse when you say that you took the appropriate action so someone else must have screwed up.
- You tell potential customers that you are the <u>vice president</u> in charge of something. When they seek out the company VP at a trade show, you tell your boss that the customers must have made a mistake.
- You work in a restaurant in which wait staff tips are shared equally, and you withhold a portion of your tips from the common pot before the tips are divided.
- You have sex with a reporting staff member and then provide special treatment to your flame.
- You take office supplies from work to use at home because you justify, you often engage in company work at home, or you worked extra hours this week, and so on.
- You spend several hours a day using your work computer to shop, check out sports scores, pay bills, do online banking, and surf the news headlines for the latest celebrity news and political opinions.
- You use up the last paper in the communal printer, and you fail to replace paper leaving the task to the next employee who uses the printer.

- You hoard supplies in your desk drawer, so you won't run out while other employees go without supplies they need to do their work.
- You overhear a piece of juicy gossip about another employee and then repeat it to other coworkers. Whether the gossip is true or false is not the issue.
- You tell a customer or potential customer that your product will perform a particular action when you don't know if it will, and you didn't check with an employee who does.
- You allow a part that you know does not meet quality standards leave your work station and hope your supervisor or the quality inspector won't notice.
- You claim credit for the work of another employee, or you fail to give public credit to a co-worker's contribution, when you share results, make a presentation, turn in a report or in any other way appear to be the sole owner of a work product or results.

This list provides examples of ways in which employees fail to practice workplace ethics (Heathfield, 2017). We can all add our own examples to the preceding list. The point is, these types of workplace ethics bring down morale, affect your coworkers negatively, and just shouldn't be practiced. We all want to work in a positive atmosphere where trust and honesty abound. It makes it a joy to go to work when people are acting appropriately and care about their coworkers. Retrieved from URL: (https://www.thebalance.com/did-you-bring-your-ethics-to-work-today-1917741)

Gallup first asked Americans to rate the ethics of certain professionals in 1976. In its latest survey, more than 1,000 adults across the country were read a list of 22 jobs and asked to rate the honesty and ethical standards of people in each as "very high," "high," "average," "low," "very low," or "no opinion." (Griswold, 2013). Check out the survey's full results below:

U.S. Views on Honesty and Ethical Standards in Professions

Please tell me how you would rate the honesty and ethical standards of people in these different fields—very high, high, average, low, or very low?

Percent saying "very high" or "high"

	Dec. 5-8, 2013
Nurses	82
Pharmacists	70
Grade school teachers	70
Medical doctors	69
Military officers	69
Police officers	54
Clergy	47
Day care providers	46
Judges	46
Nursing home operators	32
Auto mechanics	29
Bankers	27
Local officeholders	23
Business executives	22
Newspaper reporters	21
Lawyers	20
TV reporters	20
Advertising practitioners	14
State officeholders	14
Car salespeople	9
Members of Congress	8
Lobbyists	6

Retrieved from URL: (http://www.businessinsider.com/ethical-jobs-america-2013-12)

You can make your own judgments as to why some professions were rated so low. It seems politicians sink lower with each succeeding ethics poll. And as scandals make headlines in various professions, those surveyed lose faith in them. At least we can trust nurses, pharmacists, grade school teachers, medical doctors, and military officers to deal honestly.

***Great people have great values and great ethics. -- Jeffrey Gitomer

In summary, review your core values and determine what's important to you because that will morph into your attitudes and behavior. Be an ethical person that people can rely on to tell the truth and to deal honestly with everyone. People always follow someone who knows where they're going, so be a good role model.

IN-YOUR-FACE CHALLENGE

Get in touch with your values! Even if you've disgraced yourself, get back in the game and display your values and character. Don't lie down, stick up for what you believe in. Don't take advantage, live within your conscience, and know that hard work, education, and determination are the keys to success. Show your stuff and go get 'em!

References

Petty, R. E. and Cacioppo, J. T. (1981). *Attitudes and Persuasion: Classic and Contemporary Approaches*. Dubuque, IA: Brown.

Wray, R. D., Luft, R. L., and Highland, P. J. (1996). *Fundamentals of Human Relations*. Cincinnati, OH: South-Western.

Hopkins, I. (2013, October 30). Low employee morale linked to lack of communication. *HomeNews*. (https://www.hcamag.com/hr-news/low-employee-morale-linked-to-lack-of-communication-180904.aspx)

Chapter 3-Self-Esteem & Positive Reinforcement

Many psychologists agree that the most important trait a person can have is Self-Esteem. Our whole personal make-up is due to self-esteem. Our belief in ourselves, a belief that we can accomplish what we set out to do, self-confidence, ability to face challenges, how we deal with setbacks, and how we take criticism are all wrapped up in how we feel about ourselves and our abilities. Deep down, how do you feel about yourself? The amazing thing about self-esteem is that it's not set once and for all in childhood. It never stagnates and will fluctuate throughout your lifetime; however, you should have baseline self-esteem that remains constant. That's the self-confidence deep inside us that no one can ever shake. This chapter was purposely put in the middle of the book because self-esteem is at the heart of all we do.

1. Self-Esteem

***No one can make you feel inferior without your consent.
                                   -- Eleanor Roosevelt

What is Self-Esteem?

In psychology, the term self-esteem is used to describe a person's overall sense of self-worth or personal value. In other words, how much you appreciate and like yourself.

- Self-esteem is often seen as a personality trait, which means that it tends to be stable and enduring.
- Self-esteem can involve a variety of beliefs about yourself, such as the appraisal of your own appearance, beliefs, emotions, and behaviors.

Why Self-Esteem is Important

Self-esteem can play a significant role in your motivation and success throughout your life. Low self-esteem may hold you back from succeeding at school or work because you don't believe yourself to be capable of success.

By contrast, having a healthy self-esteem can help you achieve because you navigate life with a positive, assertive attitude and believe you can accomplish your goals (Cherry, 2017). Retrieved from URL: (https://www.verywell.com/what-is-self-esteem-2795868)

Signs of Healthy Self-Esteem

1. Inviting intimacy
I'm not talking about sex. I'm talking about sharing our authentic selves.

Sharing ourselves with others feels dangerous if we fear we won't measure up. **Low self-esteem makes us feel too vulnerable to let others get close.** But high self-esteem says it's okay for people to see who we really are — we're worth a look.
While many people with a poor self-image may fiercely pursue relationships, true intimacy is often lacking.

2. Actively seeking work you enjoy
There are reasons why people stay in jobs they hate. Most people will say they feel stuck, and for some, the options are genuinely limited by circumstances.

But for every person who is actually trapped in a job he or she doesn't like, there are a dozen more who stay in unsatisfying jobs through sheer inertia.

High self-esteem **encourages us to reach for the stars**, not because we're so great, or better than other people, but because we know it's perfectly natural to want to be satisfied and productive at work.

3. Valuing honesty in self and others
People with low self-esteem may use dishonesty to protect themselves or others from some real or imagined consequence of telling the truth.

Those with high self-esteem know that they can hack the consequences of telling the truth, if need be. **Dishonesty and self-esteem are like oil and water**.

Being a basically honest person takes no effort when you have integrity, which correlates with healthy self-esteem.

4. Accepting responsibility for the quality of your life
People with high self-esteem tend to have what's called an "internal locus of control." This means that **they believe in their own ability** to influence the course and character of their lives. The opposite of an internal locus of control is an *external* locus of control, which asserts that life is like a lottery; you just get sick, fired, or hit by a bus because of circumstance, and there's absolutely nothing you can do about it.

Obviously, sometimes bad things happen to good people through no fault of their own. But getting a flu shot, changing your work habits at the first sign that the boss is unhappy, and looking both ways before crossing the street are things you can do if you want to take responsibility for your life.

5. Caring about your physical health
Appropriate concern for your physical health is a sign of self-esteem because such concern is only possible if you value yourself.

To neglect abuse or otherwise mistreat your own body is to refuse responsibility for the quality of your life.

Please note that **you can't always tell who cares about their health just by looking at them**; some people who appear healthy are careless with themselves, and many people who don't meet society's standards for a "healthy" appearance are diligent in their self-care.

6. Liking children
This one's complex and controversial. Some people who don't like children might just be partial to logic, quiet, or germlessness.

But for many folks who don't like kids, it's because **being around kids puts them in touch with parts of themselves that feel small, weak or vulnerable**.

Often these people were treated without enough empathy when they were children themselves. They learned that kids don't matter, or that they're annoying, stupid, etc.
You can't enjoy healthy self-esteem if you don't value and embrace all parts of yourself, including the injured child inside.

7. Avoiding self-destructive behaviors
There are many ways to self-destruct. Addictions, poor financial decisions, reckless driving and dangerous relationships are just a few.

People who like themselves avoid situations and people that spell trouble, because **inviting trouble doesn't make sense** to those who value themselves and their quality of life.

Poor self-esteem, on the other hand, says, "Who cares? Not me. I'm not worth saving from trouble." Or even, "I *like* trouble; at least it's familiar."

Self-destructive impulses can only exist where there's not enough self-esteem. Who would want to destroy someone they truly cared for?

8. Taking calculated risks
Self-esteem seeks success, because success is a natural state for those who have a positive view of themselves and others.

To be successful, one sometimes has to take chances that can feel scary. **People with healthy self-regard are able to press forward**, even on an uncertain path, when the alternative is certain stagnation.

Their integrity demands that they strive to reach personal goals, even when the outcome isn't guaranteed. They know that the biggest regrets in life are not the things we tried that didn't work out, but the things we never tried at all.

9. Building up other people
High self-esteem is a gift to both ourselves and others. We don't have to expend precious energy defending ourselves from imagined insults to our adequacy, or belittling other people to make us feel better about ourselves.

When we feel genuinely happy with who we are, we want other people to be happy with themselves, too. Validating others comes easily when we believe our own thoughts, feelings and opinions matter. Validation strengthens relationships.

The great news about these indicators of good self-esteem is that **the signs and the self-esteem are mutually reinforcing**: If you behave consistently as if you had high self-esteem, you will raise your self-esteem. But don't take my word for it; try it yourself and see (Gilbertson). Retrieved from URL:
(http://tinagilbertson.com/self-esteem-signs/)

***If you care what other people think, you will always be their prisoner. -- Lao Tzu

Wholesome self-esteem is the conviction that one is as worthwhile as anyone else, but not more so. On one hand, we feel a quiet gladness to be who we are and a sense of dignity that comes from realizing that we share what all humans possess — intrinsic worth. On the other hand, those with self-esteem remain humble, realizing that everyone has much to learn and that we are all really in the same boat. (*10 Simple Solutions for Building Self-Esteem*, by Schiraldi). (https://psychcentral.com/blog/archives/2012/01/30/signs-of-low-self-esteem/)

The preceding quote from Schiraldi is very important to take to heart because people with healthy self-esteem need to acquire a quiet self-confidence, **not arrogance**, or a **feeling that they are better than others**.

Signs of Low Self-Esteem

Here is a list of some weird signs of low self-esteem that are easy to miss and suggestions of what to do:

1. You Apologize For Living
If someone bumps into you on the street, do you apologize? People with low self-esteem often suffer from a faulty self-image, or an inaccurate view of their worth. According to the Self-Esteem Institute, and they may genuinely feel like everything that goes wrong is somehow their fault.

What to do instead: When you hear yourself apologizing, acknowledge that the apology is inappropriate and remind yourself that you did not do anything wrong.

2. You Claim Everything Is Luck

When something great happens to you, do you say you were just lucky or blessed or in the right place at the right time? Do you take things one step further and even say you don't know why they happened because <u>you're not worthy</u>? The truth is, you probably worked your ass off to get where you are. Your talents, intelligence, and personality also played a role in your success. According to the Self-Esteem Institute, these are called <u>irrational or dishonest self-statements</u>. Other types include not accepting compliments, deflecting praise, and criticizing others who are in the same boat.

What to do instead: When someone gives you a compliment, practice simply saying "thank you." Also, why not own that you are awesome and you got that promotion because you *are* really good at what you do?

3. You Buy Things You Don't Actually Like

When you shop for clothes or decorate your apartment, do you do so with the opinions of others in mind? On a bigger scale, did you pick a major that you thought would impress your parents instead of one that would advance your dreams? Comparing yourself to others and living for approval are killers of both joy and self-esteem.

What to do instead: Stop comparing yourself to others. Columbia University's "Go Ask Alice" said, "If you can't control comparing yourself to others, <u>how about focusing on your similarities with others</u>?"

4. You Hide In Your Room

Would you rather die than be in the same apartment as a roommate who is mad at you? Are you constantly worried about others being mad at you while ignoring that you have feelings about the situation as well? <u>Avoiding conflict or saying things to appease others</u> is a sign of low self-esteem, according to Life Hack.

What to do instead: Life Hack recommended using, "an affirmation such as 'my opinion matters' or "I live authentically.'"

5. You Have That One Weird Habit
Maybe you pick at scabs or bite the skin around your nails or constantly police your body for hairs that you can pluck. According to Elements Behavioral Health, this is called compulsive self-mutilation and it's a common habit of people with anxiety or low self-esteem. It's often a coping mechanism for uncomfortable feelings.

What to do instead: Try writing your feelings down in a journal to give yourself another outlet. You may need help from a therapist to stop, according to Elements.

6. You Take More Naps Now Than You Did In Preschool
According to Margarita Tartakovsky, M.S. of *PsychCentral*, low self-esteem has a lot of physical side effects, such as fatigue. Naps could also be an avoidance tactic when you have a lot on your plate, or a sign of depression.

What to do instead: Try talking with a therapist to help improve the impact of low self-esteem on your life. You can also try practical tips, such as eating better, getting enough sleep at night, and exercising, to improve your energy.

7. You Check Your Phone for Non-Existent Messages
When there's a lull in the conversation or when you're left alone for a minute at a party, do you jump right to your phone instead of chatting or mingling? Maybe you're bored. Or maybe you're not confident enough to think that other people want to talk to you or care about what you have to say. Poor social skills can be a tell-tale sign of low self-esteem, according to The Self Esteem Institute.

What to do instead: Scan the party for acquaintances and see if there's someone you're comfortable talking to. If not, check the room for other loners and say hey or introduce yourself. You might also look for party games you can join in on. The group setting of the games might make you feel a little less on-the-spot as one-on-one conversations sometimes can.

8. You Tell Really Dumb Lies

Maybe you're trying to keep the peace or maybe you don't think the truth is interesting enough but you tell little white lies all the time. Later you're like "Oh my, why did I say that?" This is common behavior, according to The Self Esteem Institute, which points out that people with low self-esteem often wear masks or pretend to be something they're not to gain approval.

What to do instead: Let yourself be vulnerable and explore the idea that people will still like you as you reveal your truths.

9. You Can Never Pick A Place to Eat

It's the whole "what do you want to eat?" "I don't know, what do you want to eat?" conversation, amplified. Not only do people with low self-esteem have trouble making simple decisions, according to *Lifehack*, but they also frequently change their minds when they do decide something.

What to do instead: Tell yourself "seriously, though, the world isn't going to end if my friend says, 'No, I don't want Taco Bell.'"

If you find yourself doing a lot of these things, it may be time to take a good, hard look at your self-esteem. You might find that life is a lot easier (and more fun) when you're more self-assured (Newsome, 2015). Retrieved from URL: (https://www.bustle.com/articles/112199-11-weird-signs-of-low-self-esteem-that-are-easy-to-miss)

***Take care how you speak to yourself---because you are listening.

Factors Influencing Self-Esteem (how it develops)

Our self-esteem develops through three stages:

- **Childhood**. We are not born with values or self-esteem; these are characteristics that must be developed. As children, our parents and authority figures have a significant impact on us through messages they send. That's why it is so important to send positive messages to our children. If they are constantly criticized and punished, they may be prone to having low self-esteem. Of course, give the child the chance to fail but be there to help them learn from the experience.
- **Adolescence**. This stage is earmarked by academic achievement, identity development, and social acceptance. Academic achievement can result in high or low self-esteem depending on grades, friends, and involvement in school activities. Identity formation is crucial in this stage because the young person is trying to find themselves and where they fit in. Different phases include: hair style and length, tattoos, dress, role models, even musical groups that may change frequently in searching for an identity. Social acceptance can mean reputation, being accepted into a social club, making the sports team, or being accepted by a group of friends.
- **Adulthood**. We said earlier that self-esteem doesn't remain stagnant and fluctuates somewhat throughout life. As adults, we can define ourselves in three ways: what we do for a living, material possessions, or internal values. *Careers* are a status symbol and often we are judged by our work title. When we lose our job, it is very difficult because our career is our identity and we get lost. Another way to define ourselves is through the *things we own*. You may have the most expensive house on the block, or the newest car, or fastest computer, but does it really matter in the long run? If that's the source of your self-esteem, you may be

disappointed. The last and best way, to define ourselves is through *internal values* and emotional make-up. If you lose your job, or things you own, your strong internal value system can keep you moving forward in times of adversity.

How to Improve Self-Esteem

1.   Belief in God. Knowing you're not alone is a tremendous feeling. We've all heard the "Let go, let God," or "God don't make no junk," statements, but they are true. Whatever higher power you believe in, it gives you strength and hope to continue on in life. We are all unique individuals with different talents, so build your esteem from there.

2.   Small steps. You won't change overnight and suddenly have an overabundance of self-esteem. Analyze how you feel about yourself and why your esteem is low. Take small steps by reading self-help books and trying out your new found self-confidence.

3.   Build on small successes. Fall back on things you've accomplished and remember how you felt at the time. How about the time you won that award or the speech you made in school you got complimented for? Regain that swagger of yours and realize that no one can keep you down. Always come back stronger.

4.   Locus of control and choices. "A locus of control orientation is a belief about whether the outcomes of our actions are contingent on what we do (internal control orientation) or on events outside our personal control (external control orientation)," explained psychologist Philip Zimbardo in his 1985 book *Psychology and Life*.

Strive for an *internal* locus of control. That means that you control outcomes by choices you make. When you live up to your own high standards and internal values they will surpass any goals your company sets for you.

The flip-side is *external* locus of control, which means something 'outside' of you is controlling your behavior. For example, when you read your horoscope in the morning and it says that you're going to have a bad day, you call in sick to work and stay home. That's external locus of control. An internal locus of control person will read their horoscope after the workday is over to see how true it was.

5. Set goals. Goal-setting is a great way to build self-esteem because as you reach a goal you feel better about yourself. You begin focusing on goal achievement instead of your low self-esteem and benefits accrue from there. As often as you can, visualize achieving your goals. However, make sure to set goals that are challenging but not impossible to attain.

6. What are you good at? What are your strengths? What do you enjoy doing? Tap into that and build from there. The by-product will be higher self-esteem because you appreciate yourself and your abilities.

7. Learn to accept compliments. An easy tip-off to having low self-esteem is not accepting compliments. Why dismiss a compliment? When someone says, "Thanks for helping me," say, "I'm glad I could help," or "You're welcome," instead of "Oh, it was nothing." You deserve the recognition, so accept the compliment when it comes.

8. Appreciate what you have. Shouldn't we be celebrating Thanksgiving every day? Count your blessings. We live in a free society. We can make choices about what we want to do or be. Be grateful for friends, your job, your health, for learning new skills, and for having unique abilities.

9. **Positive self-talk**. We all hold internal conversations as we go through our days, and sometimes our nights. Psychologists have identified one important type of these inner monologues as "self-talk," in which you provide opinions and evaluations on what you're doing as you're doing it. You can think of self-talk as the inner voice equivalent of sports announcers commenting on a player's successes or failures on the playing field.

Unlike that sports commentary, which athletes never hear while they're competing, you can actually "hear" what your own self-talk is saying. When this is upbeat and self-validating, the results can boost your productivity. However, when the voice is critical and harsh, the effect can be emotionally crippling.

Consider what happens after you've done something embarrassing. Does your inner voice say "that was sure stupid"? How about if you haven't even done anything wrong or stupid at all, but your self-talk is just as critical? This **destructive** type of self-talk causes you to question yourself so constantly that you can soon become paralyzed with doubt and uncertainty (Whitbourne, 2013). Retrieved from URL: (https://www.psychologytoday.com/blog/fulfillment-any-age/201309/make-your-self-talk-work-you)

We all talk to ourselves at 400-600 words-a-minute every waking minute of the day. How do you talk to yourself? "It looks like another great day," or, "I wonder what problems today will bring?" Self-talk plants the seeds, positively or negatively, for your level of self-esteem. Denis Waitley, says, "The mind can't dwell on the reverse of an idea." That statement shows the importance of thinking and talking to yourself in a <u>positive</u> manner. So run towards the light, not away from the dark.

To help you rid yourself of negative self-talk and accentuate the positive, adopt these positive affirmations as your own:

I FORGIVE MYSELF
I FORGIVE ALL OTHERS
I AM MY OWN BEST FRIEND
I WILL ALWAYS BE THERE FOR MYSELF
I ACCEPT AND APPRECIATE MYSELF EXACTLY AS I AM
I SEE AND VALUE MY UNIQUENESS
I SEE OTHERS AS PRECIOUS BEINGS
I ACCEPT RESPONSIBILITY FOR MY LIFE
I TAKE GOOD CARE OF MYSELF
I ONLY SET POSITIVE STANDARDS FOR MYSELF
I RESPECT MYSELF AND MY CHOICES
I RELEASE NON-BENEFICIAL THOUGHTS AND BELIEFS
I LET GO OF MY PAST
I AM EASY ON MYSELF
I KNOW I AM DOING THE BEST I CAN (always have, always will)
I WILL ALWAYS DO MY BEST
I APPRECIATE MY LIFE BY ENJOYING IT
I WISH THE VERY BEST FOR MYSELF
I CONTEMPLATE AND MEDITATE TO KNOW MYSELF
I FOLLOW MY INNER GUIDANCE
I FOCUS POSITIVELY ON WHAT I LIKE
MY HEALTH IS VERY IMPORTANT TO ME
I LISTEN TO THE MESSAGES OF MY BODY
I TREAT MY BODY WELL
Retrieved from URL: (http://www.russellsmall.com/positive-self-talk-affirmations)

10. Draw a line in your soul. You've heard of 'draw a line in the sand,' but this is when you dig in and say, "I am a good person and I'll continue on my path, regardless of what they say or how they judge me." They've pushed you as far as you'll let them, now it's time to let the criticism and the negatives roll off your back. Keep your baseline self-esteem at all costs, but "if three people call you a jackass, get a saddle." This simply means that if one person criticizes your behavior, that's okay. If two people, then you might consider changing. But if three people criticize your behavior, then look seriously at changing. We all like to please people and if they notice something in us that we are willing to change, then it could be for the better. However, keep your self-esteem intact!

11. The company you keep. If friends aren't supportive or find fault, then find new friends. If you don't, they will drag you down. Life is tough enough without having a support group who accepts you as you are. Isn't it a pity that some, so called friends, seem to secretly enjoy it when you fail or struggle at something? Misery loves company but so does success!

12. Don't compare yourself to others. We all do because it makes us feel better about ourselves at the expense of another. It seems we have to compare ourselves favorably to someone not as fortunate. That gives us a sense of power. However, it's false power because there will always be people lesser than you and greater than you. To improve self-esteem, compete against yourself. Your goal is to constantly improve by doing better each time. For instance, if you made 10 sales last month, then next month shoot for 12 sales. Who cares how many sales a coworker made because *you are improving* and doing a good job. Achievement builds self-esteem.

13. Get competitive. This involves self-talk, not the type of behavior so often demonstrated by pro athletes who flaunt the touchdown in front of the other team. This is cognitive competition, or competing through your thought processes. For instance, I tell students who have to give a speech to not only visualize success but to think to themselves, "Sure, he gave a good speech, but wait until you hear my speech, it will knock your socks off, and you'll give me a standing ovation!" They are simply competitive, positive thoughts that you would never say out loud, but it instills the competitive spirit for self-confidence to help you succeed.

14. Make decisions. People with low self-esteem can't make up their minds. They hem-haw around, procrastinate, ask other people for advice, and they end up sitting on their hands taking no action at all. Before long the opportunity has passed so then they have the excuse that they ran out of time. Make a decision! Go ahead and get other input, do more research, but make a decision! Many decisions are self-evident if we do enough research. When we arm ourselves with more information, the answer becomes clear. Even if it's wrong, you made a decision, and with a positive attitude and hard work you can correct the error and be a better person. You are becoming more self-aware and developing healthy self-esteem!

2. Positive Reinforcement

Positive reinforcement is a very powerful and effective tool to help shape and change behavior. Positive reinforcement works by presenting a motivating item to the person after the desired behavior is exhibited, making the behavior more likely to happen in the future. Retrieved from URL: (www.nspt4kids.com/parenting/the-difference-between-positive-and-negative-reinforcement/)

***Be an encourager. The world has plenty of critics already.
-- Dave Willis.org

Why Positive Reinforcement is Important

Whether you're a child or the CEO of a corporation, we all need positive reinforcement.
It is critical to one's success and makes us feel good about ourselves. Who doesn't appreciate words of praise or a pat on the back to make them feel appreciated? In Maslow's hierarchy of needs theory, the middle three need levels are fulfilled through positive reinforcement. It fulfills safety/security needs because we believe we're a valued employee and on the right track. It also fulfills social/belongingness needs because it makes us feel like we belong. Lastly, it fulfills esteem needs because we feel more positive about ourselves.

To illustrate the importance of positive reinforcement, read the following excerpt from an interview with Bill Sims, February 12, 2014, the author of *Green Beans & Ice Cream: The Remarkable Power of Positive Reinforcement*:

Conventional wisdom has always held that cash is king when it comes to employee motivation. Companies spend trillions of dollars annually doling out bonuses and performance incentives. In addition to this you can add the "soft stuff" which runs the gamut from t-shirts, Thanksgiving turkeys, and a gold watch every 5 years of service. Quite often these approaches fail miserably. A 2007 study by the Incentive Federation, for instance, found that while gifts with a logo are one of the most commonly used employee "motivators" they are also the least effective. Why is it that the least effective motivators are the ones used most often?
In his book "1001 Ways to Recognize Employees," Bob Nelson demonstrates that the top two drivers of employee performance are: "I am able to make a difference at work" and "I have been recognized recently for what I do." Money ranks a distant fifth.

Sadly, over 68% of the workers that Nelson interviewed had never received even a simple "Thank You" from their boss in the previous six months – today, that number is creeping closer to 80%. When it comes to positive reinforcement folks, we're not getting better, we're getting worse. In further research, Nelson found that while employees rank positive feedback from their boss as the best motivator, their supervisors didn't believe that positive reinforcement mattered. During one of my leadership workshops, one supervisor joked..."Positive reinforcement? Yeah, we give them that every Friday, Bill...it's called a paycheck."

*All jokes aside, what does work, and what will always work is sincere, specific positive feedback and reinforcement. Most people think positive reinforcement consists of gifts, bonuses, or pay raises—and cash bonuses and incentive pay can play a large role in driving performance improvement, they are merely one form of positive reinforcement. You see, quite, often, the best kinds of positive reinforcement **are free**. In my book, I discuss the Neuron Study, done in Japan. It scientifically proves why and how positive verbal praise and feedback stimulate the same neural pathways that cash stimulates.*

It doesn't cost you one penny to tell your kids, spouse, employees, and co-workers that they did something right. So why don't we do it more often? The irony is, that the thing workers say they need the most, is the thing they receive the least—genuine positive reinforcement and feedback. Retrieved from URL: (https://www.quickbase.com/blog/the-importance-of-positive-reinforcement-in-the-workplace)

In the workplace, supervisors can use positive reinforcement for purposes such as increasing productivity and improving the morale of an individual or a department. It does the following four things for employees and the workplace:

- **Providing sense of worth**. Providing positive reinforcement can give an employee a sense of self-worth. This can be important in instances where areas that need improvement have been pointed out previously, such as during a performance appraisal. Positive reinforcement lets the employee know she is making progress and that management is recognizing her efforts. This can also help to alleviate any self-doubts she may be having about her ability to perform well.

- **Encouraging good behavior**. Positive reinforcement can increase the chances of a desired behavior reoccurring in the future. When workers receive repeated praise or encouragement for good performance, they're more likely to continue performing well. For example, a habitually tardy employee who receives praise for arriving at work early may seek to continue the pattern if he continues to receive positive feedback from his supervisor.

- **Improving workplace morale**. Positive reinforcement can help improve morale in the workplace. A supervisor who lets workers know she appreciated their efforts can foster a more positive work atmosphere. Employees may not only be happier and more productive in their own position, but they also may be more willing to help others who may be overworked or struggling. This is especially important in work environments where teamwork is essential to getting the job done or when employees work in close proximity to each other.

- **Fitting in**. New employees may have concerns about fitting in with the culture of the workplace and whether they are demonstrating the ability to perform as desired. Positive reinforcement early on in the training or orientation process can alleviate these concerns and help the employee relax and feel more confident about her ability to be successful. It can also encourage her to feel more comfortable about asking questions or expressing concerns as her training progresses (Joseph). Retrieved from URL:

(http://smallbusiness.chron.com/positive-reinforcement-important-workplace-11566.html)

Power of Praise and Recognition

A study, funded by Make Their Day, an employee motivation firm, and Badgeville, a gamification company, surveyed 1,200 U.S. employees from a broad cross-section of industries. Among the study's highlights:

- 83% of respondents said recognition for contributions was more fulfilling than any rewards or
  gifts;
- 76% found peer praise very or extremely motivating;
- 88% found praise from managers very or extremely motivating;
- 90% said a "fun work environment" was very or extremely motivating.

"Workers of all ages, especially the rising Millennial population," concluded Ken Comee, Badgeville CEO, "are motivated by real-time feedback, fun, engaging work environments, and status-based recognition over tangible rewards."

People leave managers, not companies. In general, the study reinforced the centrality of the manager-employee relationship in employee engagement. It underscored the importance of the emotional element of an employee's commitment to an organization, as opposed to the financial aspect. As the saying goes, "People leave managers, not companies." Usually for emotional, not financial, reasons (Lipman, 2013). Retrieved from URL: (https://www.psychologytoday.com/blog/mind-the-manager/201306/new-employee-study-shows-recognition-matters-more-money)

Still need convincing of the importance of recognition and praise? Consider the following excerpt from Rath & Clifton's, *How Full Is Your Bucket*, 2004 :

The concepts of "recognition" and "praise" . . . are two critical components for creating positive emotions in organizations. In fact, [The Gallup Organization] has surveyed more than 4 million employees worldwide on this topic. Our latest analysis, which includes more than 10,000 business units and more than 30 industries, has found that individuals who receive regular recognition and praise:

- increase their individual productivity
- increase engagement among their colleagues
- are more likely to stay with their organization
- receive higher loyalty and satisfaction scores from customers
- have better safety records and fewer accidents on the job . . .

Of course, there's a flip side. Right now, the majority of us don't give or receive anywhere near the amount of praise that we should. As a result, we're much less productive, and in many cases, completely disengaged in our jobs. According to the U.S. Department of Labor, **the number-one reason people leave their jobs** is because they "do not feel appreciated." Retrieved from URL: (http://news.gallup.com/businessjournal/12157/power-praise-recognition.aspx)

The Beauty of Positive Reinforcement

Positive reinforcement is contagious because when someone compliments us it cheers us up and we are more likely to pass on positive reinforcement to others.

The other unique quality of positive reinforcement is that we can easily see when it's needed. It is readily discernible when someone is asking for praise or a compliment. Why not give them the recognition they are looking for? The simplest example is with children. If they are learning to play a musical instrument, for example, they want their parents to listen to them. That's because they want their parents to compliment them, whether they are good or not. It's positive reinforcement that tells the child he is accepted, that someone is paying attention to him, and that his efforts are rewarded. We need that as adults, also!

Guess what? Positive reinforcement doesn't cost you or your employer a thing! But it pays off big time!

***What is love except another name for the use of positive reinforcement? Or vice versa. -- B.F. Skinner

Why don't we use Positive Reinforcement more?

There are so many opportunities to give positive reinforcement to people around us. It enhances our lives, makes us feel valued, and motivates us to put forth our best efforts. Then why isn't it used more? Here are some common barriers to positive reinforcement:

- **Preoccupation with self.** This is commonly known as *narcissism.* A narcissist is someone who is vain or egotistical and only concerned about themselves. When you're preoccupied with yourself and trying to climb the corporate ladder for that big promotion you don't have the time or inclination to compliment others. You are self-absorbed and you feel that nobody is your equal. **An idea:** try to think of others and think about how you crave positive reinforcement. It's easy to appreciate people when you'd like the same appreciation.
- **The "too busy" syndrome.** This is related to narcissism because you feel you're so busy that you must be important and you just don't have the time to positively reinforce other people. Everyone's trying to get ahead and with work

piling up, deadlines to meet, and general job pressures, it's easy to postpone giving a deserved compliment or praise. **An idea**: if you were to die tomorrow, who are the people closest to you that you'd like to thank? Then take time to do that very thing today!

- **Pride**. Some of us are too proud. We worked our way to the top the hard way, so why do we owe anyone positive reinforcement? "I did it on my own and no one ever recognized or complimented me!" As professionals we tend to think that new hires can find their way on their own and giving compliments and encouragement may show we are weak. **An idea**: giving deserved positive reinforcement to someone shows your strength, not your weakness. You will be revered as someone who encourages others.

- **Not knowing what to say or do**. Sometimes we don't know exactly how to give positive reinforcement, so we don't. It's easier to ignore giving recognition or appreciation than it is to come up with ways to show them. Or, maybe the boss has already recognized them so you shouldn't have to. Yes, you should! If they are your friend or coworker they will be waiting, hoping that you'll recognize them in some way. Even if it's a quick "well done," it will be meaningful to them. **An idea**: stretch yourself in finding ways to reinforce others, whether it's a card, email, or sticky note. It doesn't take much time and it will pay big dividends.

- **Misconceptions about positive reinforcement**. Some bosses feel that if they show appreciation to their employee, that the employee will demand something in return. That's bull! When you thank someone it makes them feel more valuable to the organization. They won't turn around and ask for a raise. We all have cravings for compliments, to be appreciated, to be recognized, and to be validated as human beings.

Have you ever thought about complimenting the boss? We don't have the power to give them a raise, but appreciation is free and probably longer lasting. It doesn't have to be daily recognition because the positive reinforcement may lose its effectiveness. For example, in the great song writing team of Lennon & McCartney, Paul said that when John paid him a compliment, it meant something, because he didn't give compliments often. **An idea**: try complimenting someone and see if they demand anything in return.

IN-YOUR-FACE CHALLENGE

Be good to yourself, rise above life's clutter and maintain your healthy self-esteem. A sign of healthy self-esteem is helping others, so thank someone this week who has given their time to assist you. Show them you appreciate them!

Volunteer to help at a charity so you'll realize how lucky you are to be alive, healthy, employed, and living in a free society!

Chapter 4 – Motivating

***It does not matter how slowly you go as long as you do not stop. -- Confucius

<u>What is Motivation?</u>

Motivation is a theoretical construct used to explain behavior. It represents the reasons for people's actions, desires, and needs. Motivation can also be defined as one's direction to behavior or what causes a person to want to repeat a behavior and vice versa. A motive is what prompts the person to act in a certain way, or at least develop an inclination for specific behavior. Retrieved from URL: (https://en.wikipedia.org/wiki/Motivation)

That's the definition that Wikipedia gives us, but a more useable definition is that motivation is *an internal drive towards a goal or goals.* The first part talks about *an internal drive*, which means that motivation is largely internal. In order for true motivation to occur you have to see if for yourself. Sure, we can motivate other people, but only in the short term. *Internal* motivation is long-term, and *external* motivation is short-term.

How long does your money last when you receive a raise? Only long enough to adjust your standard of living and expectations, then you need another raise. That's why money is only a short-term motivator. Or, it could be a coach at halftime promising his young team ice cream if they go out and win the second half. Again, it's short-term motivation.

If you are determined to get an education and you know it will lead to a better life, you may take two part-time jobs to help pay for tuition, but you will do what it takes to get that education. That is long-term motivation because you've internalized your goal of getting an education.

The second part of the motivation definition … *towards a goal or goals,* is fulfilling what you want to obtain or achieve. You have internalized wanting an education and you are actively working toward getting that degree (goal).

Ask yourself if you'd rather work with someone who is motivated, has a good attitude, but lacking in skills. Or, someone who is highly skilled who is not motivated and has a poor attitude. Most of us want to work with motivated coworkers. Everyone is trainable and if they are motivated they will succeed. Now, forget the other person and ask yourself if you're motivated to do a good job.

<u>Maslow the Guru</u>

Abraham Maslow's (1943, 1954) *Hierarchy of Needs* gives direction as to how we fulfill our needs as humans. He called it a hierarchy because it is a progressive model based on moving up, or progressing up, the pyramid of needs. We have unsatisfied needs that motivate us to want to satisfy those needs, so we start at the bottom at **Physiological** needs. These are our survival needs, or things we need to live, such as food, water, and shelter. Note that as each need, or level is fulfilled, it no longer motivates so we will move on to the next level, which is **Safety-Security**. On the job these needs could be medical benefits, a retirement plan, and even job stability. At home, it could be a supportive environment, owning property, or just being physically safe.

Self-actualization
(striving to reach one's potential, includes: creativity, challenges, goals)

Esteem
(self-confidence, respect, recognition)

Social-Belongingness
(friends, teamwork, family, sexual intimacy)

Safety-Security
(being physically safe, job security, job benefits stable work environment)

Physiological
(food, shelter, clothing, water, sex, breathing)

The next need level is **Social-Belongingness**, because we all need friends and family. We are social beings. These needs also include teamwork on the job and being accepted as a coworker. **Esteem** needs deal with our self-respect and also respect from others, types of recognition, and self-confidence. After we've satisfied all other needs, we climb to **Self-actualization** needs, where we strive to reach our potential. This is the level where a lot of our dreams and creativity reside. We like challenges, setting goals, and developing as human beings.

As a need is fulfilled, it no longer motivates and one can be in more than one need category at the same time, but one need will always be more powerful. And his model is flexible, not set in stone with unyielding categories. A good example is salary. Salary could fit into Physiological needs for buying food, clothing, and so on. It could also fit into Safety-Security needs for helping you buy things that make you feel more secure, such as a home, a car, or having a savings account. The third need category that could fit with salary is Esteem. Salary could be a status symbol that projects recognition or respect.

Be aware that Maslow built his theory based on a typical human beings motivation because you can find instances where people jump levels. That's okay, not everyone fits into the mold, but most of us do. For example, your friend may want to live on a mountain and be a hermit. In this case, he is circumventing the bottom three need levels and heading for Esteem and Self-actualization. Maslow believed his hierarchy was certainly valid but understood that one size doesn't fit all.

Also, Maslow's hierarchy doesn't end with Self-actualization because we constantly move up and down the need levels. Have you ever read about a business entrepreneur who is very successful and sells the venture, only to start another one? That sounds crazy to you and me. Why wouldn't the entrepreneur take the profit, sit back and enjoy life? Because he or she was not truly self-actualized and is motivated by challenge and goals rather than making money, so they're up for another challenge of starting a new business.

Overachievers fit well into the Self-actualization need level because reaching one goal is not enough. They constantly strive. They finish high school and want the college degree. They may want more than one degree. They go to work and want to self-actualize by volunteering to head up projects or committees while building the reputation that they are reliable and enthusiastic about what they do. They are respectful and courteous while they are achieving goals. You can take it from here, but you can easily see that person will be successful.

The need hierarchy theory can be used in business or at home. In business, you might determine what the employee's needs are and where they are in the hierarchy, and then provide opportunities for them to fulfill the next need levels. Or, at home, what needs can you help fulfill in your children or spouse? Charitable organizations are built around the need hierarchy. For example, when you see a homeless person, you usually don't start reading scriptures to them (self-actualization) because they're hungry. So you start at the bottom of the hierarchy and get them some food (physiological). Working up from there, you might talk about getting them shelter and later on, employment (safety-security).

Maslow's theory is fluid and can be used many ways to help ourselves and others. It helps you evaluate where you are and what you need at any stage of life. His theory is the foundation upon which many motivation theories are built and is still applicable today.

Acquired needs theory

David McClelland's research from the 1940s identified three acquired needs that he considers central to understanding human motivation. He called these needs **acquired needs** because he believed that the needs are acquired during your life. The **need for achievement** is the desire to do something better or more efficiently, to solve problems, or to master complex tasks. The **need for power** is the desire to control other people, to influence their behavior, or to be responsible for them. The **need for affiliation** is the desire to have friendly and warm relations with other people.

McClelland encourages managers to learn how to recognize the strength of these needs in themselves and in other people. Because each need can be associated with a distinct set of work preference, his insights offer helpful ideas for designing jobs and creating work environments that are rich in potential motivation.

Importantly, McClelland distinguishes between two forms of the power need. The need for *personal power* is exploitative and involves manipulation purely for the sake of personal gratification. As you might imagine, this type of power need is not respected in management. By contrast, the need for *social power* is the positive face of power. It involves the use of power in a socially responsible way, one that is directed toward group or organizational objectives rather than personal ones. This need for social power is essential to managerial leadership (Schermerhorn & Bachrach, 2016).

Need for achievement.
- *Positive* – you want that college degree, that promotion, that certificate to put on your wall, or to be recognized. We stay motivated by achieving and accomplishing things.
- *Negative* – sometimes we overachieve at the expense of others. Being single-minded towards achieving a goal can cost you friendships or hurt feelings. Try to temper your focus so that other things are not left by the wayside at the expense of your achievement.

Need for power.
- *Positive* – you desire to work your way up in the organization so you'll have the power to help others and to change policies for the better.
- *Negative* – you're power hungry so you can order people around and be the all-powerful "Oz." People have to march to your orders and you're not going to stoop to help others. Let them learn the hard way, the way you had to!

Need for affiliation.
- *Positive* – you get charged up when you're on a team and have good friends to socialize with. Office parties are good and you enjoy going to lunch with coworkers.
- *Negative* – you like to socialize to get the juicy gossip or to be able to manipulate people using information.

Which of the three needs drives you? Certainly, all three will motivate us at different stages of our lives, but which one currently motivates you to be your best? This give important insight into the kind of person you are or want to be.

Goal-setting theory

In 1960's, **Edwin Locke** put forward the Goal-setting theory of motivation. This theory states that goal setting is essentially linked to task performance. It states that specific and challenging goals along with appropriate feedback contribute to higher and better task performance.

In simple words, goals indicate and give direction to an employee about what needs to be done and how much efforts are required to be put in.

The important **features of goal-setting theory** are as follows:

- The willingness to work towards attainment of a goal is the main source of job motivation. Clear, particular and difficult goals are greater motivating factors than easy, general and vague goals.

- **Specific and clear** goals lead to greater output and better performance. Unambiguous, measurable and clear goals accompanied by a deadline for completion avoids misunderstanding.

- Goals should be **realistic and challenging**. This gives an individual a feeling of pride and triumph when he attains them, and sets him up for attainment of the next goal. The more challenging the goal, the greater is the reward generally and the more is the passion for achieving it.

- Better and appropriate feedback of results directs employee behavior and contributes to higher performance than absence of feedback. Feedback is a means of gaining reputation, making clarifications and regulating goal difficulties. It helps employees to work with more involvement and leads to greater job satisfaction.

Advantages of Goal Setting Theory

- Goal-setting theory is a technique used to raise incentives for employees to complete work quickly and effectively.

- Goal-setting leads to better performance by increasing motivation and efforts, but also through increasing and improving the feedback quality.

Limitations of Goal-Setting Theory

- Very difficult and complex goals stimulate riskier behavior.
- If the employee lacks skills and competencies to perform actions essential for goal attainment, then the goal-setting can fail and lead to undermining of performance.
- There is no evidence to prove that goal-setting improves job satisfaction.

Retrieved from URL: (http://managementstudyguide.com/goal-setting-theory-motivation.htm)

Goal-setting theory applies to us personally, it's not just for setting goals at work. We can set personal goals for finances, education, exercise, public service, and so on. Goals are motivational because as we are working towards a goal, we feel good about our accomplishments along the way. As we get closer to achieving them we become more focused and determined, since we're almost there. The key to goal setting is to make the goal challenging, but if it is too challenging you'll lose sight of it. Pick a worthy goal that might take a week to several years to reach and set benchmarks along the way to reward yourself as you reach those mini-goals. The reward need not be a new car, but something simple, yet meaningful to you. For instance, a candy bar you haven't had in a long time might be in order for losing 10 pounds, on your way to your goal of losing 25. A one-time splurge won't hurt you and will keep you motivated. Before you know it, you'll have obtained what you set out to do. Congratulations, you did it!

Equity theory
Behavioral psychologist, John Stacey Adams, developed a useful model for explaining why employee perceptions about fairness

matters. Equity Theory (Adam's Equity Theory, 1963) explains the thought process an employee uses to determine the fairness of management decision making. The core of equity theory says that individuals judge the fairness of their treatment based on how others comparable to them are treated. Employees make social comparisons to others who are similarly situated in the organization.

Said another way, an employee asks himself the following: Based on what I am giving to this organization (inputs), am I getting the same rewards (outcomes) as others are getting who give similar inputs? Equity theory says that employees view a situation as equitable when employees who give similar inputs receive similar outcomes. When the rewards differ for the same degree of effort, employees view the situation as inequitable.

Equity theory shows that inequities (perceived or real) harm employee motivation. Employees who feel that they are receiving inequitable treatment will be emotionally motivated to gain equity. What does this behavior look like? When inequities persist, employees may do any of the following:

- Decrease inputs (devote less time, do less work)
- Push for more output from the company (more pay, authority)
- Go into survival mode (do their job and little more)
- Become resistant (act out on other issues)
- Become overly competitive (focus on reducing the outputs of others)
- Quit (Tanner, 2017)

Retrieved from URL: (https://managementisajourney.com/equity-theory-why-employee-perceptions-about-fairness-do-matter/)

Don't deny it, we all compare ourselves to others and Adams simply put words to it. We compare with coworkers to make sure their salary is not out of line with ours. If it is, there are usually repercussions. We may behave in the following ways when we find a coworker with the same education and experience is making more money than we are:

- "I'm not going to work as hard and heck with staying late to finish my work; they don't pay me enough so I'm leaving at 5 p.m. sharp!" (decrease inputs)
- "I'll talk to the boss about a raise or promotion." (push for more output)
- "Time to just put my head down; do my job and my job only. I won't volunteer again for any extra assignments." (go into survival mode)
- "That new policy is really stupid and I'll tell them so, I won't change what I'm doing." (become resistant)
- "I'll work circles around my coworkers and show management they should be paying me more. But I'm not helping anyone else anymore when they get behind." (become overly competitive)
- "I'm giving my two week notice in the morning. I won't work for a company that plays favorites." (quit)

What Motivates You?

***The secret of getting ahead is getting started. -- Mark Twain

Have you ever posed this question to yourself, *"What motivates me in life?"*
So what motivates you and what makes you wake up each morning?
What drives you and why do you go through life each day?

If you are like ordinary people, you have no idea what motivates you. You don't know why you want to wake up each morning, and you don't know what you want to do with your life.

Ordinary people wake up each morning because they have to go to work. And the reason they get to work is that they want to get paid. They want to pay their bills and expenses.

In other words, **they are working for the money**. This is why when they have a choice; they choose to run away from their work. They will choose to sleep longer and sleep later when they do not have to report to the office.

Most people spend a minimum of 8 hours a day at their work. And if you work because you want to make money to pay your bills, but you are not fulfilling your calling, you will never have the motivation in life.

1. Money and Rewards
Do I need to say more? As I have explained above, most people thought that what they want in life are monies and the next shiny objects, but what they never realized is that the physical things that they want are just the means to an end.

What they are truly after is the feeling of owning the items.

Thus, if you are <u>chasing for money</u> and the rewards, think twice. What do you truly want? Is it the money? Or is it the feeling?

When you understand what you are truly after, you will value the journey more. You will appreciate the progress and process more because those are what truly count, not the end result. This is why people say that **success is a journey, not a destination**.

It is your hard work and the effort you put forth that make you who you are today. It is the journey that shapes you into the person you want to be, not the physical items.

Money is just the reward you get when you win the game, but what makes you win the game is the progress.

So **focus on the progress** and not the end result. What you have gone through is more important than what you have achieved in the end.

2. Desire to be The Best

Some people just cannot accept being number two in their lives. They fight hard and they work hard because they hate to lose.

People such as Warren Buffet and Usain Bolt are good examples. They just hate losing.
Why do you think Muhammad Ali worked so hard? Because he desired to be the champion.

"I hated every minute of training, but I said, 'Don't quit. Suffer now and live the rest of your life as a champion.'" – Muhammad Ali

Their desire to be the best is so strong that they are willing to go all out and give all their best to achieve the number one status.

They sacrifice their time and work hard every single day to become the best. **Are you willing to do that?**

Are you willing to sacrifice your weekend or your nighttime to work on your dreams? Are you willing to wake up at 5 a.m. each morning so that you can have a head-start on others?

3. Helping the Others

Some people are motivated by helping others. They want to see changes in people's lives and they want to fight for a better future for the world.

These are philanthropists, and they are willing to give up a huge portion of their wealth to make the world a better place.

In 2010, Bill Gates and Warren Buffett announced the <u>Giving Pledge campaign</u> to recruit and inspire wealthy people of the world to give a majority of their wealth to philanthropy.

When they first launched the campaign, there were as much as 40 people that joined the campaign and have pledged $125 billion for charity purposes. As of March 2016, the campaign has recruited 142 members.

These are the people who are motivated and driven to help others and to make the world a better place. They are inspired to change other people's lives.

While not everyone is driven to help others, but if you are, it is good.

You just need to understand what motivates you so that you can **channel your energy through the right platform** and achieve greater success in life.

4. Power and Fame

There is another group of people who are motivated by power and fame. Politicians are a great example here.

These are the people who are inspired to become a leader and they are driven to achieve greater power and fame in life.

They want to lead and bring their company, their people and their nation to greater heights.

What about you? Do you chase power and fame? Do you start your business to achieve what you want or because you feel good in leading your team?

You have to know what you truly desire deep within yourself.

5. Recognition

Recognition is another factor that makes certain people motivated. They want to prove that either they are right or someone is wrong.

They want the recognition for themselves or others. Do you know how Lee Iacocca achieved his recognition through reviving Chrysler in the 80s?

It is said that Ford Motors fired Lee and he felt so angry that he wanted to build a company to rival Ford. As a result, he joined Chrysler, which was in trouble at that time.

Lee then led Chrysler to become a great automobile company again. Although Chrysler went bankrupt in 2009, it has truly shown that Lee Iacocca's drive for recognition and to prove himself was a strong force for achieving success in life.

There was another similar story about Thomas Watson, who used to work for a company called NCR. Tom Watson was fired there and he wanted to prove his ex-company was wrong.

After that, Tom Watson joined a smaller company called CTR and grew it to become what is known as IBM today. He has led IBM for 40 years and has turned it into one of the leading technology companies.

So do you desire to be recognized? Do you want to prove yourself or prove that someone is wrong?

6. The Passion
The final factor that motivates most people in life is passion. Why do you think all of the successful people do what they do? Why do you think they are willing to wake up early and work harder than ordinary people? The answer is that they are passionate about what they do.
Think about it, there are times when you feel so motivated for something that you are willing to sacrifice your leisure time for it.

Maybe it's your favorite sport? Maybe it's when you got the chance to travel somewhere you love?

Whatever the reason, I believe that you understand the power of passion. When you are so passionate about something, you will think about it all the time. **You will be willing to wake up early and sacrifice your sleep for it.**

This is why passion is important because it can drive you each day to achieve what you want in life.

Sadly, most people never develop their passion in their work. They work like a zombie without feeling any passion. They make sure they are not the first one to reach the office and not the last one to leave.

No wonder most people are just plain ordinary. You are reading this because you want to be extraordinary and you want to accomplish great things in your life (Shawnlim, 2016). Retrieved from URL: (http://stunningmotivation.com/what-motivates-you-in-life/)

What motivates you in life is something you need to discover if you want to achieve remarkable success.

***If you can dream it, you can do it. -- Walt Disney

What Science says about Motivation

Employees, spouses, kids — what does it take to get people motivated so you don't have to nag them? Motivation is powerful. **It predicts success better than intelligence, ability, or salary.**

When tested in national surveys against such seemingly crucial factors as intelligence, ability, and salary, level of motivation proves to be a more significant component in predicting career success. While level of motivation is highly correlated with success,

importantly, the source of motivation varies greatly among individuals and is unrelated to success (Bashaw & Grant, 1994).
Take a look at the following research that espouses 4 steps, backed by science, to motivation.

1) Stop Bribing Them
When actors would ask the great film director Alfred Hitchcock "What's my motivation?" he would reply, "Your salary."

Rewards definitely <u>work</u>.

Rewards just motivate people to get rewards.

When the rewards go away, people stop.
And if you want anything other than basic manual labor — **if you want creative work or analytical work — rewards can actually backfire.**
Yes, you need to pay people but you should pay them just enough to take the issue of money off the table. For complex tasks we're more motivated by the need for autonomy, mastery and purpose.

2) Make Them Feel Something
We often talk about people being motivated by revenge, jealousy, fear, passion… What do these have in common?
Yeah, they're all feelings. And they're all powerful motivators.

We rarely do anything we don't feel and it's very hard to resist things we do feel. It's <u>how your brain is structured</u>.

Chip and Dan Heath sum up the research in their book *Switch: How to Change Things When Change Is Hard:*

Focus on emotions. Knowing something isn't enough to cause change. Make people (or yourself) feel something.
We often think of the workplace as less emotional, more formal and serious. And as far as motivation goes, *that's a terrible idea.*

...the core of the matter is always about changing the behavior of people, and behavior change happens in highly successful situations mostly by speaking to people's feelings.

So what's the most powerful thing for people to be feeling if you want to increase motivation?

3) Emphasize Progress
Harvard's Teresa Amabile's research found that **nothing is more motivating than progress.**

This pattern is what we call the progress principle: of all the positive events that influence inner work life, the single most powerful is progress in meaningful work; of all the negative events, the single most powerful is the opposite of progress—setbacks in the work. We consider this to be a fundamental management principle: facilitating progress is the most effective way for managers to influence inner work life.

Life satisfaction is 22 percent more likely for those with a steady stream of minor accomplishments than those who express interest only in major accomplishments. – Orlick 1998

You want a steady amount of challenge, achievement and feedback:

Progress is powerful. Encourage people to reflect on how far they've come and the good work they've done.

So you made them feel something. You demonstrated progress. How do you keep the motivation flowing?
4) Form a Cult (Well, Almost)
Not literally. No funky robes or animal sacrifice necessary. But **what *else* unites a cult?**

Looking at the research: What gives life meaning? <u>Stories</u>. What gives work meaning? <u>Stories</u>.
What creates unity and morale? <u>Stories</u>:

Institutions that can communicate a compelling historical narrative often inspire a special kind of commitment among employees. It is this dedication that directly affects a company's success and is critical to creating a strong corporate legacy...

One of the reasons Lincoln was such a good president was because <u>he was a great storyteller</u>.
Barker, Eric. (2014, April 8). How to Motivate People: 4 Steps Backed by Science. *Time*.
(<u>http://time.com/53748/how-to-motivate-people-4-steps-backed-by-science/</u>)

Common Myths about Employee Motivation

The topic of motivating employees is extremely important to managers and supervisors. Despite the importance of the topic, several myths persist -- especially among new managers and supervisors. Before looking at what management can do to support the motivation of employees, it's important first to clear up these common myths.

1. Myth #1 -- "I can motivate people"
Not really -- they have to motivate themselves. You can't motivate people any more than you can empower them. Employees have to motivate and empower themselves. However, you can set up an environment where they best motivate and empower themselves. The key is knowing how to set up the environment for each of your employees.

2. Myth #2 -- "Money is a good motivator"
Not really. Certain things like money, a nice office and job security can help people from becoming less motivated, but they usually

don't help people to become more motivated. A key goal is to understand the motivations of each of your employees.
3. Myth #3 -- "Fear is a damn good motivator"
Fear is a great motivator -- for a very short time. That's why a lot of yelling from the boss won't seem to "light a spark under employees" for a very long time.

4. Myth #4 -- "I know what motivates me, so I know what motivates my employees"
Not really. Different people are motivated by different things. I may be greatly motivated by earning time away from my job to spend more time my family. You might be motivated much more by recognition of a job well done. People are not motivated by the same things. Again, a key goal is to understand what motivates each of your employees.

5. Myth #5 -- "Increased job satisfaction means increased job performance"
Research shows this isn't necessarily true at all. Increased job satisfaction does not necessarily mean increased job performance. If the goals of the organization are not aligned with the goals of employees, then employees aren't effectively working toward the mission of the organization.

6. **Myth #6 -- "I can't comprehend employee motivation -- it's a science"**
Nah. Not true. There are some very basic steps you can take that will go a long way toward supporting your employees to motivate themselves toward increased performance in their jobs (McNamara). Retrieved from URL: (https://managementhelp.org/leadingpeople/motivating-others.htm)

IN-YOUR-FACE CHALLENGE

Now dig deep to discover what truly motivates you. (No, it's not money—think deeper).

When you know what motivates you, reflect on your *values*. What do you value most? What's important to you?

Okay, now look at your *attitude*. Does it fit well with your values and your motivation?

Then get ready because you're speeding down the freeway to success! Congratulations!

References

Schermerhorn, J. & Bachrach, D. (2016). *Exploring Management*. Wiley publishing, pp. 238-9.

Chapter 5 – Conflict Management & Emotional Control

The world we live in has become more conflict-oriented, and in order to help resolve conflicts, we need emotional control. There are examples of disagreements, disputes, and name-calling in the daily news. Oftentimes, they are accompanied by childish behavior, bullying, and power-plays in order to win. This chapter stresses the importance of learning to resolve conflicts in an emotionally controlled manner. Being able to deal with conflict in an open, honest manner while controlling your emotions is at the heart of positive human relations.

1. Conflict Management

***Dialogue is the most effective way of resolving conflict.
-- Tenzin Gyatso, The 14th Dalai Lama

Conflict and Confrontation

Wherever there are people, there always will be conflict. Conflict and confrontation often occur together. Neither is very pleasant, but both are part of our work and home lives. **Conflict** is generally defined in the dictionary as "a serious disagreement or argument, typically a protracted one." Synonyms include: dispute, squabble, quarrel, or disagreement. Whereas, **confrontation** is generally defined in the dictionary as "a hostile or argumentative meeting or situation between opposing parties." Synonyms include: conflict, clash, encounter, or face off.

From these definitions, we can easily see how conflict and confrontation are used interchangeably. However, there is a difference because conflict can be part of confrontation but we will use confrontation by itself. In the context of this book we will use confrontation, but not as 'physical' confrontation. Everyone has conflicts but sometimes you need to confront the other person to resolve the conflict. Confronting the other person involves sitting down face-to-face, communicating and airing our grievances in order to resolve the dispute. Conflict and confrontation is really no problem when it's with a friend or acquaintance because if it goes unresolved we will simply write them out of our lives. But what do we do when it's a co-worker we have to see every day, or a family member? That's when we need to learn ways to resolve our differences, or at least co-exist. If not, become an MMA fighter and stop reading this book, because you don't need it!

***Conflict is inevitable, but combat is optional. -- Max Lucado

Causes of Conflict

According to psychologists Art Bell and Brett Hart, there are eight common causes of conflict in the workplace. Bell and Hart identified these common causes in separate articles on workplace conflict in 2000 and 2002.

1. Conflicting Resources
We all need access to certain resources – whether these are office supplies, help from colleagues, or even a meeting room – to do our jobs well. When more than one person or group needs access to a particular resource, conflict can occur.

If you or your people are in conflict over resources, use techniques such as Win-Win Negotiation to reach a shared agreement (we'll talk later about this approach). You can also help team members overcome this cause of conflict by making sure that they have everything they need to do their jobs well. Teach them how to prioritize their time and resources, as well as how to negotiate with one another to prevent this type of conflict.

If people start battling for a resource, sit both parties down to discuss openly why their needs are at odds. An open discussion about the problem can help each party see the other's perspective and become more <u>empathic</u> about their needs.

2. Conflicting Styles

Everyone works differently, according to his or her individual needs and personality. For instance, some people love the thrill of getting things done at the last minute, while others need the structure of strict deadlines to perform. However, when working styles clash, conflict can often occur.

To prevent and manage this type of conflict in your team, consider people's working styles and natural <u>group roles</u> when you build your team.

You can also encourage people to take a personality test, such as the <u>Myers-Briggs Personality Test</u>. This can help them become more accepting of other people's styles of working, and be more flexible as a result.

3. Conflicting Perceptions

All of us see the world through our own lens, and differences in perceptions of events can cause conflict, particularly where one person knows something that the other person doesn't know, but doesn't realize this.

If your team members regularly engage in "turf wars" or gossip, you might have a problem with conflicting perceptions. Additionally, negative performance reviews or customer complaints can also result from this type of conflict.

Make an effort to eliminate this conflict by communicating openly with your team, even when you have to share bad news. The more information you share with your people, the less likely it is that they will come up with their own interpretations of events.

Different perceptions are also a common cause of office politics. For instance, if you assign a project to one person that normally would be someone else's responsibility, you may unwittingly ignite a power struggle between the two. Learn how to navigate office politics, and coach your team to do the same.

4. Conflicting Goals

Sometimes we have conflicting goals in our work. For instance, one of our managers might tell us that speed is the most important goal with customers. Another manager might say that in-depth, high-quality service is the top priority. It's sometimes quite difficult to reconcile the two!

Whenever you set goals for your team members, make sure that those goals don't conflict with other goals set for that person, or set for other people.

And if your own goals are unclear or conflicting, speak with your boss and negotiate goals that work for everyone.

5. Conflicting Pressures

We often have to depend on our colleagues to get our work done. However, what happens when you need a report from your colleague by noon, and he's already preparing a different report for someone else by that same deadline?

Conflicting pressures are similar to conflicting goals; the only difference is that conflicting pressures usually involve urgent tasks, while conflicting goals typically involve projects with longer timelines.

If you suspect that people are experiencing conflict because of clashing short-term objectives, reschedule tasks and deadlines to relieve the pressure.

6. Conflicting Roles

Sometimes we have to perform a task that's outside our normal role or responsibilities. If this causes us to step into someone else's "territory," then conflict and power struggles can occur. The same can happen in reverse – sometimes we may feel that a particular task should be completed by someone else.

Conflicting roles are similar to conflicting perceptions. After all, one team member may view a task as his or her responsibility or territory. But when someone else comes in to take over that task, conflict occurs.

If you suspect that team members are experiencing conflict over their roles, explain why you've assigned tasks or projects to each person. Your explanation could go a long way toward remedying the pressure.

7. Different Personal Values

Imagine that your boss has just asked you to perform a task that conflicts with your ethical standards. Do you do as your boss asks, or do you refuse? If you refuse, will you lose your boss's trust, or even your job?

When our work conflicts with our personal values like this, conflict can quickly arise. To avoid this in your team, practice ethical leadership: try not to ask your team to do anything that clashes with their values, or with yours.

There may be times when you're asked to do things that clash with your personal ethics.

8. Unpredictable Policies

When rules and policies change at work and you don't communicate that change clearly to your team, confusion and conflict can occur.

In addition, if you fail to apply workplace policies consistently with members of your team, the disparity in treatment can also become a source of dissension.

When rules and policies change, make sure that you communicate exactly what will be done differently and, more importantly, why the policy is changing. When people understand <u>why the rules are there</u>, they're far more likely to accept the change.

Once the rules are in place, strive to enforce them fairly and consistently. Retrieved from URL: (<u>https://www.mindtools.com/pages/article/eight-causes-conflict.htm</u>)

<u>Conflict Management Styles</u>

Conflict management is the practice of being able to identify and handle conflicts sensibly, fairly, and efficiently. Since conflicts in a business are a natural part of the workplace, it is important that there are people who understand conflicts and know how to resolve them. This is important in today's market more than ever. Everyone is striving to show how valuable they are to the company they work for and at times, this can lead to disputes with other members of the team.

Conflict Management Styles
Conflicts happen. How an employee responds and resolves conflict will limit or enable that employee's success. Here are five conflict styles that a manager will follow according to Kenneth W. Thomas and Ralph H. Kilmann:

An **accommodating** manager is one who cooperates to a high degree. This may be at the manager's own expense and actually work against that manager's own goals, objectives, and desired outcomes. This approach is effective when the other person is the expert or has a better solution.

Avoiding an issue is one way a manager might attempt to resolve conflict. This type of conflict style does not help the other staff members reach their goals and does not help the manager who is avoiding the issue and cannot assertively pursue his or her own goals. However, this works well when the issue is trivial or when the manager has no chance of winning.

Collaborating managers become partners or pair up with each other to achieve both of their goals in this style. This is how managers break free of the win-lose paradigm and seek the win-win. This can be effective for complex scenarios where managers need to find a novel solution.

Competing: This is the win-lose approach. A manager is acting in a very assertive way to achieve his or her own goals without seeking to cooperate with other employees, and it may be at the expense of those other employees. This approach may be appropriate for emergencies when time is of the essence.

Compromising: This is the lose-lose scenario where neither person nor manager really achieves what they want. This requires a moderate level of assertiveness and cooperation. It may be appropriate for scenarios where you need a temporary solution or where both sides have equally important goals (Mckinney). Retrieved from URL: (https://study.com/academy/lesson/what-is-conflict-management-definition-styles-strategies.html)

At the beginning of this chapter, we asked what you could do when you're in conflict with a coworker you have to work with every day. This is the time to confront the person to clear the air. It may simply be a communication problem and one of you may have misinterpreted the meaning of the message. Potential conflict averted. If no agreement can be reached, then appeal to the greater good. Tell them "I know we don't agree on things, but can we put our personality differences aside while we work so that we can get the product out?" As an employee, you don't have to be best friends with everyone and you may never want to go to happy hour with that person. Most of us don't get to choose who we want to work with. That's okay, but putting the pettiness aside and working to get the job done properly from 9 to 5, could benefit you both.

<u>Three Behavior Types</u>

Communication breakdowns are a common cause for conflict, and poor communication strategies can lead to a rapid escalation. Likewise, effective communication strategies can help you correct these miscommunications to move conflicts quickly towards resolution.

One idea that can help you choose the best communication strategy for the situation comes from the communication continuum.

The continuum runs from passive strategies on the left to aggressive strategies on the right. In passive strategies, you communicate in a way that protects the other person's interests at the expense of yours. Aggressive strategies represent the other extreme where you communicate in a way that protects your interests at the expense of the other person's.

| Passive | Assertive | Aggressive |

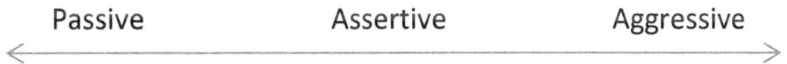

Assertive communication strategies lie in the middle. These strategies depend on approaches that protect the interests of both parties in the communication – yours and the other person's.

Assertive communication approaches represent a range of techniques rather than a single point on the continuum. Some of the approaches lie a little to the left of middle – they are a little more passive – and other approaches lie a little to the right of middle – they are a little more aggressive. Wherever they lie on the continuum, all assertive strategies have this in common – the interests of both parties are protected. Depending on the situation, you might choose to go a little more passive or a little more aggressive within the assertive range.

Whether it sits a little left of center or a little right of center, the guiding principle behind all assertive communication techniques is that the technique allows you to effectively express your needs and concerns in a way that respects the needs and concerns of the other person.
Here are some guidelines for communicating **assertively**...

Use "I" statements.
State your perspective as your perspective or interpretation without resorting to statements that blame the other person. For example, "You made me angry" is aggressive, while "I felt angry" is assertive.

Focus on behaviors.
Avoid the desire to slip into interpretations like calling the other person rude or insensitive. Comment on their behaviors or words without labeling them.

Keep your responses short.
The longer you talk, the more likely you are to slip into either passive or aggressive techniques.

Monitor your tone of voice and non-verbal messages.
You can choose just the right words and ruin it with a sharp tone or aggressive posture.

Listen.
Pay close attention to what they have to say as well. If you do not listen, you will become aggressive.

Maintain appropriate eye contact.
Too little eye contact and you could be perceived as dishonest. Too much eye contact and you could come across as aggressive. In most situations in North America, relatively steady eye contact with brief breaks every few seconds is probably appropriate (Harris). Retrieved from URL: (https://recoveringengineer.com/resolving-conflict/the-difference-between-passive-aggressive-and-assertive-communication/)

While working on becoming more assertive don't forget to start with small steps and climb from there. For instance, if someone keeps the thermostat too cool in the office, rather than demanding they turn the heat up, try saying "I feel uncomfortable when the temperature is too cool, can we try a degree or two higher?" By using "I" statements, you are telling the person how you feel and you're not in attack mode. Being assertive is a much better way to get your needs met. A passive person won't say anything and probably freeze or bring a sweater to work. On the other hand, an aggressive person will turn the thermostat to their liking whether others like it or not. More than likely, this will result in conflict.

***Conflict cannot survive without your participation.
                                                        -- Wayne Dyer

In a conflict situation, whether at work or at home, remember that passive behavior will result in you not sticking up for your rights and getting run over. Using assertive behavior means that you *stand up for your rights in a way that does not violate the rights of others.* Lastly, aggressive behavior starts out like assertive, but crosses the line. It is behavior where you *stand up for your rights in a way that violates the rights of others.*

Strategies

While many people think of negotiations as a competition where one side wins and the other loses, in reality, negotiations involve a more complex mixture of winning and losing. The outcome of almost all two party negotiations can be categorized as **win-lose** (one party benefits to the detriment of the other), **lose-lose** (both parties are worse off after the negotiation), or **win-win** (both parties come out ahead). If the negotiation fails, no agreement has been reached and the parties are forced to seek alternative solutions.

Win-Lose

Frequently in win-lose scenarios, both sides have attempted to win, without much regard for the outcome of the other party. Both parties may have come into the negotiation with a desired goal and a "walk away" point. In a win-lose scenario, one party falls within this target range (or even exceeds it) and the other party falls below their target range.

Notice that win-lose outcomes occur when the losing side can be pushed below their "walk away" point. This can happen when the losing side doesn't know what their best alternative is to reaching an outcome in the negotiation, or where they keep negotiating against their own interest. Many other factors, like coercion and asymmetric information can also lead to win-lose outcomes.

Lose-Lose

In a lose-lose scenario both parties concede bargaining positions outside their target ranges. If the negotiators fail to reach an agreement, both parties may end up in worse positions than when they started the negotiations, this is often included as a lose-lose outcome.

If one or both parties can't walk away from a negotiation, but are unwilling to make concessions, both will be forced to deal with the poor consequences of not reaching an agreement. Alternatively, both parties could be too quick to make concessions, reaching a compromise that is fair, but detrimental to both sides. Likewise, if both parties are mistaken about the benefits of what the other side is offering, they may reach an agreement they later come to regret.

Win-Win

In a win-win scenario, both parties end up, at minimum, within their target ranges. This could simply be reaching a fair middle ground that both parties benefit from, or it could mean finding a creative new solution that improves the position of both parties.

If both parties come to the table with goals that are mutually compatible, there is a good chance that the negotiation can result in a win for both sides. Of course, there is nothing that prevents a negotiator from trying to press an advantage and push the other side into a losing position, but there is a risk in that case that the other side will walk away from the negotiation.

Win-win results are the most stable outcomes of negotiations; since both parties are happy with the result, they have little reason to back out at a later time. Both parties have an incentive to negotiate with each other again, laying the foundation for a mutually beneficial working relationship (Martinez). Retrieved from URL: (http://www.storyboardthat.com/articles/b/win-win-negotiation)

The important lesson to remember from these strategies is that anything with "lose" in the title will only be a short-term, or temporary, fix. Why? Because there's at least one loser in the mix. In the win-lose strategy, the loser wants to come back stronger next time in order to win. Really nothing has been settled long-term.

The lose-lose strategy is often used in labor-management negotiations. Both sides want to avoid a strike so they employ an arbitrator to decide the issue. The arbitrator may decide that both parties have to give concessions in order to obtain a fair settlement. Now, both sides want to come back stronger next time to get those concessions back. Really nothing has been settled long-term. A side note: Some homeowners and car insurance policies provide for arbitration if there is a claim dispute.

Of course, the win-win strategy is a long-term solution as both parties feel they've gained something from the negotiations. Be aware that for the win-win strategy to be effective both parties must be open-minded, with no hidden agendas or the strategy won't work. It is a tough, but worthwhile strategy that should always be pursued.

But wait! In our society, the win-win strategy can be next to impossible to achieve. Think back on how you were raised. We are raised competing for our parent's attention. Then we go to school and compete for grades, boyfriends and girlfriends, and on sports teams to be the champions. As we get older, we compete for jobs and promotions. We all want to be number one! "I win, you lose," is the way of American life. So you can see the challenges involved, but the win-win strategy is doable. However, it must be done honestly, candidly, and with both parties goals in mind.

Conflict Resolution

Many conflicts are brought about by miscommunication and it's imperative that you are certain what the other person is saying. Some of us have a quirky sense of humor, and some of us have no sense of humor at all. Have you ever kidded with someone and they thought you were serious? If you aren't sure the other person knows you are joking, then tell them. For instance, "…I'm joking," or "…I'm only kidding." That may solve the problem right there because there actually is no conflict, just misunderstanding brought on by miscommunicating. It also gives a chance for apologies when miscommunications occur. Feedback what the other person is saying so that it gives a chance for both sender and receiver to make sure the message is understood. However, if you're satisfied it is a true conflict and not a misunderstanding, then consider the following tips:

- **Get your point across**. We previously discussed the importance of assertiveness in getting your point across. Did you say what you intended to say? Are people looking quizzically at you and possibly don't understand everything you've said? Sometimes in the heat of discussion we say things the wrong way or choose the wrong word. If that happens, quickly correct what you've said, apologize if necessary and continue on. Make certain you have presented your side well by using clear communication and your positive human relations skills. Aggressive behavior or language will only take you further from your goal of resolving the conflict.

- **Listen**. Actively listen to the other person, don't "pretend listen," while you're thinking of a counterargument. Chances are you'll then miss the point of what the other person is saying. You've told your side of it so now it's your turn to listen and focus on the other person's point of view.

- **Think before speaking**. It takes a few seconds to digest information and to carefully choose your words. Organize your thoughts. Have you ever just blurted out words and had to apologize later? When you're trying to resolve a conflict, saying the wrong thing may hurt feelings and add to the problem.

- **Stay calm and soften your language**. Swearing at the other person puts them on the defensive and does not impress. It is definitely not professional. By the same token, getting angry is not an option either. If you get red-faced with flailing arms, then learn techniques for anger management (see Emotional Maturity). Take a break, make sure you're sitting and not standing, admit when you're wrong, be honest, use "I" statements, breathe, and don't stare but maintain eye contact.

- **Save the other person's face**. Respect the other person, don't stoop to name-calling, let them save face and don't bring up hurtful accusations. Emotions are inevitable but try to stick to the facts as much as you can. Play fair, don't act like a member of Congress!

- **Don't negotiate like a car dealer**. If you're going to "low-ball" the other person (not give them the value and respect they deserve, or try to blow smoke), the other person will see through it and the negotiations will become more difficult. Be open and above board in your communications and make sure you've gotten your point across clearly.

- **Roleplay**. This is an effective technique to invoke empathy and help you realize where the other person is coming from. When you're looking at the conflict from another person's perspective it brings valuable insight into negotiations.

- **Use humor appropriately**. Humor can be an obstacle to conflict management if it's used inappropriately. Sometimes it can break the tension, but it depends on the seriousness of the conflict. If the other person does not have a sense of humor, don't use it. They may perceive that you are either not taking things seriously or that you're making fun of them.

- **Compliment them**. Complimenting them might sound crazy, but if they have a strength that you admire bring it to their attention. You might start off by saying, "You always look at all the facts and make good decisions," or, "I appreciate that you always play fair." Any compliments could help negotiations toward resolving the conflict.

There are several conflict resolution strategies in research literature, but most have the following steps in common on how to reach a successful conclusion:

1. **Define the problem**. Take time to truly investigate and define the problem. It's an old cliché that "when you define the problem, you're halfway to the solution." But it's true! For instance, suppose there's a dispute about the company selling shoddy products. When you ask the first assembly-line foreman, he says, "Hey,

garbage in, garbage out, we can't make a quality product without quality parts to build it with." When you ask the second assembly-line foreman, he says, "It's the line employees, nobody wants to work and do a good job anymore." When you ask the third assembly-line foreman, he says, "The assembly line is always breaking down and needs replacing, it's putting us behind and we have to take short cuts to catch up." In this case, the problem has not been defined yet. Get input from teams, individuals or bosses and pinpoint the conflict or problem that needs to be addressed.

2. **Collect facts and opinions**. In the case of an organization, gather facts from all participants involved in the conflict. For example, if two employees were fighting in the warehouse, then find out the following: Who are they? How big is the conflict? How long has each been with the company? Have they been in conflict before? What are their work records? Have they both had a performance review recently? After all facts are gathered, opinions should also be considered. Not only by those in the dispute but coworkers and possibly other bosses. The goal is to get as complete a picture as possible of the entire conflict so that it can be satisfactorily resolved. In the case of personal conflicts, have each person list their concerns and they can list facts as well as opinions at this stage. Have you ever had to make an important decision but don't have enough information? You know that more research will make the decision more evident. Again, by gathering as much information as possible, it's easier for the conflict to be resolved.

3. **List alternative solutions**. This is the "brainstorming" step where any solution can be listed without judgment (at least not now). Numbering alternatives can help simplify the process for the next step in

conflict resolution. For example, an employee instigated a fight in the warehouse, so some alternatives might be: do nothing, promote the employee, fire the employee, send them for retraining, enroll them in anger management, put them on probation, transfer them, etc. Trying to be creative and realistic at the same time will enhance the quality of ideas. Get as many alternatives listed as possible because no matter how far out one alternative may seem, it might end up being part of the final resolution.

4. **Evaluate alternatives**. In the previous step, you numbered possible solutions. Now, use the "If...then..." approach to whittle down to the best ones. For instance, "If we do alternative #1, then this is likely to happen." "If we do alternative #2, then this is likely to happen." Evaluating the alternatives with this approach helps take emotions out of the equation and you will always make better decisions if you can put your emotions aside.

5. **Select the "best" alternative(s)**. Sometimes the best resolution to the conflict may involve a combination of two or more alternatives. Looking back to the example of the employee fighting (step 2); our final resolution to the conflict might be to combine putting him on probation with requiring attendance at an anger management seminar.

2. Emotional Control

What is Emotional Control?

Emotional self-control is the ability to manage disturbing emotions and remain effective, even in stressful situations. Notice that "manage emotions," is different from suppressing emotions. We need our positive feelings—that's what makes life rich. But we also need to allow ourselves the space and time to process difficult emotions, but context matters. It's one thing to do it in a heartfelt conversation with a good friend, and entirely another to release your anger or frustration at work. With emotional self-control, you can manage destabilizing emotions, staying calm and clear-headed.

To understand the importance of emotional self-control, it helps to know what's going on in our brain when we're not in control. In his book, *The Brain and Emotional Intelligence*, Daniel Goleman, explains:

"The **amygdala** is the brain's radar for threat. Our brain was designed as a tool for survival. In the brain's blueprint the amygdala holds a privileged position. If the amygdala detects a threat, in an instant it can take over the rest of the brain—particularly the prefrontal cortex—and we have what's called an **amygdala hijack**.

During a hijack, we can't learn, and we rely on over-learned habits, ways we've behaved time and time again. We can't innovate or be flexible during a hijack.

The hijack captures our attention, beaming it in on the threat at hand. If you're at work when you have an amygdala hijack, you can't focus on what your job demands—you can only think about what's troubling you. Our memory shuffles, too, so that we remember most readily what's relevant to the threat—but can't remember other things so well. During a hijack, we can't learn, and we rely on over-learned habits, ways we've behaved time and time again. We can't innovate or be flexible during a hijack.

… the amygdala often makes mistakes…. while the amygdala gets its data on what we see and hear in a single neuron from the eye and ear—that's super-fast in brain time—it only receives a small fraction of the signals those senses receive. The vast majority goes to other parts of the brain that take longer to analyze these inputs—and get a more accurate reading. The amygdala, in contrast, gets a sloppy picture and has to react instantly. It often makes mistakes, particularly in modern life, where the 'dangers' are symbolic, not physical threats. So, we overreact in ways we often regret later."

***Emotional maturity is when a person hurts you, and you try to understand their situation and don't hurt them back.

How to develop Emotional Self-Control

How can we minimize emotional hijacks? First, we need to use another emotional intelligence competency, **emotional self-awareness**. That starts with paying attention to our inner signals—an application of mindfulness, which lets us see our destructive emotions as they start to build, not just when our amygdala hijacks us.

If you don't notice your amygdala has hijacked the more rational part of your brain, it's hard to regain emotional equilibrium until the hijack runs its course. It's better to stop it before it gets too far. To end a hijack, **start with mindfulness**, monitoring what's going on in your mind.

Notice "I'm really upset now" or "I'm starting to get upset." If you can recognize familiar sensations that a hijack is beginning—your shoulders tense up or your stomach churns—it is easier to stop it.

Then, you can try a cognitive approach: talk yourself out of it, reason with yourself. Or you can intervene biologically. Meditation or relaxation techniques that calm your body and mind—such as **deep belly breathing**—are very helpful. As with mindfulness, these work best during the hijack when you have *practiced them regularly*. Unless these methods have become a strong habit of the mind, you can't invoke them out of the blue (Goleman, 2017). Retrieved from URL: (https://www.mindful.org/emotional-self-control-matters/)

The key is to recognize the "hijack" is occurring, meaning that you're getting angry. That's why so many people say to "breathe, try to relax, count to 10," when dealing with anger. It's true that when you're angry you can't think, or you certainly can't think rationally. When your "red-eyed monster" has you in his grip of anger and rage, there's no way you can think straight.

So if you ever find yourself tossed around helplessly on a hysterical tumultuous sea of emotion and want some ways to at least adjust your sails, here are seven suggestions:

1) Control your emotions by looking ahead
An old Zen master said: "Your anger, depression, spite, or despair, so seemingly real and important right now; where will they have gone in a month, a week, or even a moment?"
Very intense emotions blind us to the future and con us that now is all that matters. In fact, when we are incredibly angry or anxious, we can even momentarily forget that there is even going to *be* a future. There was an employee who'd stuffed an ice cream cone in his boss's face when he was enraged. This momentary action had huge and prolonged consequences on this man's life; particularly finances.

We've all said or done things we later regret simply because, for a time, we let ourselves be dictated by our own emotion. If you get angry, think to yourself: "How will I feel tomorrow if I lose my dignity and tell this person (I have to see every day) that they have a face like a cow patty?" If you are anxious about some imminent event, say to yourself: "Wow, how am I going to feel tomorrow/next week when I look back at this?" Look beyond the immediate and you'll see the bigger picture and calm down, too.

2) Get to know yourself
We all kid ourselves a little, or a lot. "No, I'm really pleased for you! No, I *really am!*" (Arghhhhhhhh!)

Learn to observe your own attitudes and emotional ebbs and flows. One key first step to emotional control is to know when we are actually *being* emotional and also why.

If you catch yourself feeling unexpectedly strongly about something, ask yourself why. Controlling your emotions isn't about pretending they are not there. If you feel jealous, angry, sad, bitter, or greedy, label exactly how you are feeling in your own mind: "Okay, I don't like that I'm feeling this way, but I'm feeling very envious!" Now you've admitted it to yourself.

The next step is to identify *why* you feel the way you do: "I hate to admit it, but I'm feeling envious of Bob because he's just gets too many compliments for his work and I don't!"

Being able to exercise this self-honesty means you don't have to resort to what a large proportion of the human race does. You won't have to 'rationalize'. We rationalize by kidding ourselves that we are angry with someone not because they have got a raise at work and we haven't, but because of 'their attitude towards us' or some other made up reason. Knowing *what* emotion you are feeling and being man or woman enough to identify the truth as to why you are feeling it means you're that much closer to doing something about it.

3) Change your mood; do something different
We tend to assume that moods just 'happen to us' and, like storms, the best we can do is wait until they pass. But, unlike climatic storms, we *can* influence - even change - our moods without resorting to unhealthy means such as alcohol or drugs. Being able to manage and influence your own emotions is a powerful marker for good health, emotional maturity, and happiness.

One way to alter your mood is to instantly do something else. For example, if you feel flat and bored, continuing to watch uninteresting TV will deepen the mood. Switching it off and going for a walk in a new neighborhood will *inevitably change your mood*. If you feel cross, consciously focus on three things in your life for which you can feel grateful. If you are anxious, start to imagine that what you are anxious about has already happened and gone much better than expected.

The important thing is just to do or think something different. Don't be passively carried along by the current of the mood. The quickest way to do this may be to simply imagine *not* feeling the way you are feeling. So if I'm feeling hacked off, I might close my eyes and take a few moments to strongly imagine feeling relaxed and comfortable and even in a good mood. This will, at the very least, neutralize the bad mood and may even put you in a good mood.

4) Observe how others deal effectively with their emotions
We can learn so much from other people (as long as we look to the *right* people to learn from!).

How do other 'emotionally skilled' people deal with their frustrations and difficulties? You could even ask them: "How do you keep so cool when you're presenting to all these people? Why doesn't that make you angry? How do you keep smiling after such setbacks?"

Their answers could actually change your life if you start to apply what you learn.

5) Change your physiology
Some people assume that emotions are 'all in your head', whereas actually all emotions are *physical* responses. Anger pushes heart rate and blood pressure up, which is why having an angry temperament is a predictor of heart disease; anxiety produces lots of physical changes; and even depression suppresses the immune system.

So part of changing your emotional state involves dealing directly with the physical changes. Physical changes are led by the way we breathe. For instance, anger and anxiety can only 'work' if we are breathing quicker with shallow breaths. Take time to:

- Stop breathing for five seconds (to 'reset' your breath).
- Now breathe in slowly, focusing on your diaphragm, until your lungs are full of air.
- Then breathe out *even more slowly* (and whilst doing this, imagine that you are breathing pure rest and relaxation into your hands).
- Keep doing this and remember it's the *out-breath* that will calm everything down.

6) Use your noggin

Think of emotion as a strong but stupid being that sometimes needs your guidance and direction. We *need* some emotion to motivate us, but it needs to be the right emotion at the right time applied in the right way. The more emotional we become, the stupider we become. This is because emotions want us to react blindly and physically rather than to think or be objective and rational.

Being objective and rational when a lion was attacking wouldn't have been great from an evolutionary point of view - because it would have slowed us down. But much of modern life needs measured calm thought rather than blind and sloppy emotional responses.

7) Create spare capacity in your life

We experience counterproductive emotions for different reasons. Maybe we have never learned to control ourselves or perhaps we are living in such a way that makes it *more likely we'll experience emotional problems.*

To be emotionally healthy, a person needs to:

- Feel safe and secure; feel they have safe territory.
- Regularly give and receive quality attention.
- Feel a sense of influence and control over their life.
- Feel part of a wider community.
- Enjoy friendship, fun, love, and intimacy with significant people.
- Feel a sense of status; basically, feel they have a recognizable role in life. This also connects to a sense of competence and achievement.
- Feel stretched but not stressed to avoid stagnation, boredom, and to enhance self-esteem and a sense of status in life.

When these are met adequately, we then feel our life has meaning and purpose.

Not meeting basic needs leaves us feeling that life is pointless and meaningless and will leave us wide open to emotional problems.

When you live in a way that, to some extent, meets all or most of the above needs, then you'll enjoy greater emotional stability and control. *Knowing* what you need in life is the first step to creating 'spare capacity' to focus *beyond* your emotions. And you can see how *not* meeting the need for feeling secure or getting enough attention or feeling connected to people around you could cause you emotional problems. Really think about these needs and gradually pursue activities that are likely to help you fulfill them (Tyrrell). Retrieved from URL: (http://www.uncommonhelp.me/articles/how-to-control-your-emotions/)

What about Emotional Intelligence?

Emotional intelligence (EI), or emotional quotient (EQ), is the capacity of individuals to recognize their own, and other people's emotions, to discriminate between different feelings and label them appropriately, and to use emotional information to guide thinking and behavior.
Retrieved from URL:
(https://en.wikipedia.org/wiki/Emotional_intelligence)

Emotionally intelligent people use self-awareness to their advantage to assess a situation, get perspective, listen without judgment, process, and hold back from reacting head on. At times, it means the decision to sit on your decision. By thinking over your situation rationally, without drama, you'll eventually arrive at other, more sane conclusions.

It's being able to look at the whole picture and both sides of an issue; it's having the ability to tap into someone else's feelings (as well as your own) to consider a different outcome; this overlaps into another key element of emotional intelligence: empathy. Daniel Goleman, a leader in the field of emotional intelligence research, once said:

If you don't have self-awareness, if you are not able to manage your distressing emotions, if you can't have empathy and have effective relationships, then no matter how smart you are, you are not going to get very far.

According to Goleman, **self-awareness** is the key cornerstone to emotional intelligence. In fact, a number of studies have proven self-awareness as a success factor. In one study undertaken by Green Peak Partners and Cornell University examining 72 executives with revenues from $50 million to $5 billion, it was found that "a high self-awareness score was the strongest predictor of overall success." (Schwantes, *Inc.*) Retrieved from URL:

(https://www.inc.com/marcel-schwantes/the-1-masterful-trait-of-people-with-high-emotional-intelligence.html)

Emotional Maturity

So instead of focusing on emotional intelligence, perhaps we would be better served by focusing on emotional maturity.

The difference between the two is important. Emotional maturity is not "intellectual" but refers to a higher state of self-awareness – something that lies beyond "intelligence" - where we are guided by our senses, intuition and heart.

Emotional maturity is characterized by five principles:
1. Every negative emotion we experience is a childhood emotion overlaid on a current person,
    circumstance, place, event or object.
2. Emotionally, many adults are 3-4-5-year-old children in adult bodies.
3. No one can make you feel a way you don't want to feel.
4. An adult can be emotionally mature and child-like or immature and childish.
5. Mindfulness, focus and presence are the keys to emotional maturity.
Emotional maturity focuses on our emotional history, beginning with our interactions with our primary caregivers, extended family, teachers, friends, etc. We learn that around the age of seven, our psychological and emotional "programming" is set. Our emotional reactivity (anger, sadness, fear, shame, hurt, guilt, loneliness, etc.) that was triggered early on in life becomes stored in our cells and arises when "related" triggers pop up later in life (Vajda, 2013).
Retrieved from URL: (http://www.management-issues.com/opinion/6811/emotional-intelligence-or-emotional-maturity/)

<u>But I'm still angry!</u>

What factors make us susceptible to anger? One is an accumulation of built-up stresses. That's why your temper can flare more easily after a frustrating day. The second is letting anger and resentments smolder. When anger becomes chronic, cortisol, the <u>stress</u> hormone, contributes to its slow burn. Remaining in this condition makes you edgy, quick to snap. Research has proven that anger feeds on itself. The effect is cumulative: each angry episode builds on the hormonal momentum of the time before. For example, even the most devoted, loving mothers may be horrified to find themselves screaming at their kids if they haven't learned to constructively diffuse a backlog of irritations. Therefore, the powerful lesson our biology teaches us is the necessity of breaking the hostility cycle early on, and that brooding on the past is hazardous to your well-being.

***Holding onto anger is like drinking poison and expecting the other person to die. – Buddha

For optimal <u>health</u>, you must address your anger. But the point isn't to keep blowing up when you're upset rather--it's to develop strategies to express anger that is body-friendly.
Otherwise, you'll be set up for illnesses such as migraines, irritable bowel syndrome, or <u>chronic pain</u>, which can be exacerbated by tension. Or you'll keep jacking up your blood pressure and constricting your blood vessels, which compromises flow to the heart. A Johns Hopkins study reports that young men who habitually react to stress with anger are more likely than their calmer counterparts to have an early heart attack, even without a family history of heart disease. Further, other studies have shown that hostile couples who hurl insults and roll their eyes when arguing physically heal more slowly than less antagonistic partners who have a "we're in this together" attitude.

Still, repressing anger isn't the answer either. Research also reveals that those who keep silent during marital disputes have a greater chance of dying from heart disease or suffering stress-related ailments than those who speak their minds.

Here are four tips to productively cope with anger in daily life:

1. When you're upset, pause, and slowly count to ten.
To offset the adrenaline surge of anger, train yourself not to lash back impulsively. Wait before you speak. Take a few deep breaths and VERY slowly, silently, count to ten (or to fifty if necessary). Use the lull of these moments to regroup before you decide what to do so you don't say something you regret

2. Take a cooling-off period.
To further quiet your neurotransmitters, take an extended time-out, hours or even longer. When you're steaming, retreat to a calm setting to lower your stress level. Reduce external stimulation. Dim the lights. Listen to soothing music. <u>Meditate</u>. Do some aerobic exercise or yoga to expel anger from your system.

3. Don't address anger when you're rushed.
Make sure you have adequate time to identify what's made you angry. A Princeton study found that even after theology students heard a lecture on the Good Samaritan, they still didn't stop to help a distressed person on the street when they thought they'd be late for their next class. Thus, allotting unhurried time to resolve the conflict lets you tap into your most compassionate response.

4. Don't try to address your anger when you're tired or before <u>sleep</u>.
Since anger revs up your system, it can interfere with restful sleep and cause <u>insomnia</u>. The mind grinds. Better to examine your anger earlier in the day so your adrenaline can simmer down. Also being well rested makes you less prone to reacting with irritation and allows you to stay balanced.

The goal with anger is to own the moment so this emotion doesn't own you. Then you can mindfully respond rather than simply react.

You'll have the lucidity to be solution oriented and therefore empower how you relate to others (Orloff, 2011). Retrieved from URL: (https://www.psychologytoday.com/blog/emotional-freedom/201102/four-strategies-cope-anger-in-healthy-way)

One last method to deal with anger is to sleep on it. The conflict or anger is often the result of a simple miscommunication and some books say to address it as soon as it occurs. That advice says to get it out in the open and deal with it immediately. This might be a valid approach for some people, but I disagree with that advice. I have to sleep on it because if I confront the person immediately after the event I'll more than likely say something I'll regret in the heat of the moment. Of course, then apologies are in order. If you let the conflict "breathe," that is, give it time and thought, then you'll be much better prepared to resolve the problem. This is not a passive approach and you're only giving it 24 hours to digest and analyze the situation before proceeding. Remember that you're only getting some breathing and thinking time to help deal with the conflict. When you wake up the next morning, if it's still on your mind and it bothers you, then confront the person to get the issue resolved. But you have to get back to resolving it! Sometimes couples tend to say "we'll discuss this further when we both get home from work," and they don't follow up. It then results in the hostility growing until someone blows up over it because the conflict was never satisfactorily dealt with. Get it out, deal with it, and move on. This is part of emotional maturity!

Many times you or another person are angry and mask the problem. Later, some little thing sets you off on a tirade that's not even the issue. For example, when I buy my wife things she likes to eat, sometimes she doesn't eat it and it sits in the refrigerator until the food is spoiled. I have to throw it out and then I confront her about wasting food and wasting money, but the real issue was something that occurred days before when she questioned my money management methods. This is childish because it's not honest communication. I should have told her that she hurt my feelings because I've always prided myself on managing our finances, but I didn't. I waited and griped about wasting $3 worth of food. We need to deal with the issue at hand before it gets out of hand. The other person may not know what they did to offend you and if you don't tell them then it's your problem to solve and no one else's!

IN-YOUR-FACE CHALLENGE

Deal with the conflict upfront! Don't back away or ignore it because it will only get worse. It doesn't go away until you deal with it. Live a healthy life by resolving conflicts before they fester and end up exploding.

Learn emotional maturity and analyze all options before making choices. You will never regret it and you'll sleep much better at night!

Summary

***Live to satisfy, Love without condition, Laugh
     uncontrollably, Dream wildly. Pursue
     happiness and never give up!

There should be a major emphasis on communication because it's
no joke; it is the basis for everything! Certainly it's easier said than
done but that doesn't mean we should give up trying to improve
communications. It is difficult to communicate with the boss or
your spouse, but keeping in mind the variables in the
communication process will help you be a more attentive, effective
communicator. To improve your communication skills, illicit
feedback to become more self-aware.

What about expectations? Are your expectations being met? Do
you voice them properly? Do you meet others expectations? It is a
worthy exercise to sit down with people you work with and people
you love and explain expectations you have of them. If we don't let
people know our expectations we end up feeling hurt or used, but
it's our own fault! If people don't know what you expect of them
then they guess and usually miss the mark. There's nothing to hide
here. You're not disclosing too much of yourself, you're simply
voicing what you expect. Be candid and your expectations will be
met!

It is obvious you have a well-developed value system or you
wouldn't be reading this book. But always look to reinforce those
values by treating people with respect and not letting your values
erode. It is comforting to know that we are on the right track, so
check your values occasionally. It's always helpful to hang around
people with similar values to reinforce each other. You know right
from wrong so act accordingly. Don't cheat yourself and don't
cheat other people. Live up to the wholesome reputation of being
known to keep your word and that you can be trusted. If you've
done someone wrong, step up immediately with a sincere apology

so you can be forgiven and move on. Never bend to trends of half-truths, name-calling, or acting unprofessionally. It can be a career buster!

Self-esteem fluctuates but you should have a baseline of confidence in your abilities that enables you steady sailing in troubled waters. There will be continuous challenges and we all make mistakes, but be good to yourself. Don't be so critical and give yourself a break. You'd give others the same consideration so it's time you gave yourself that same consideration. Realize life's ups and downs and know that tomorrow will be a better day and that the roller coaster will go back up before the ride is over. Strive to achieve, better the world, better yourself, and in the process your healthy self-esteem will keep you progressing successfully throughout your lifetime.

It seems when you positively reinforce someone they not only appreciate it but they're more prone to return that positive reinforcement and even pass it on to others. We all need positive reinforcement. It lends stability to our lives. Recognition and praise go well beyond a paycheck. People gravitate towards people and organizations that appreciate hard work and recognition is critical to that process. It's not manipulative to tell someone that you sincerely appreciate what they did. It will pay dividends!

Are you motivated? If you're not then find a way to get yourself going. Dream of a better life and how to get there so you can plant the seeds for success and happiness. Set a goal. Determining what motivates you, along with knowing your core values, will lead you to a career that's right for you! Never give up, just find another way. If you're living for the paycheck, then find another job that you enjoy. If you hate your job then stop griping about it and make a change. Find work where you can grow as an individual and keep your skills up-to-date. When you're a valued employee because of your abilities and potential, then you'll never be out of work!

Conflict is like stress, we can't get rid of it and we must learn ways to manage it. Use proper means for negotiating and resolving the conflict fairly. The first step is always to determine if miscommunication is involved. If it is, it can be cleared up before it gets to true conflict status. Use the confrontation technique to sit down with an open mind, listen, and work for mutual benefit. Try for the win-win approach so everyone can profit, or at least learn from the process.

In this world of people "losing it," and behavior being manifested through violence, emotional maturity is a must. Rise above the fray and realize human emotions can be tempered with good judgment, logic, and sincerity. If anger overwhelms you, then deal with it constructively. If you don't, it may impair your health. High blood pressure, weaker immune system, and heart disease is definitely too high a price to pay for getting angry. Go to the gym, go for a run, sit quietly and reflect—do whatever it takes to dissipate the anger. If not, it can cost you a relationship or a job or your life.

Finally: DECIDE. COMMIT. SUCCEED.

Author's Notes

Education is the greatest equalizer known. The value of education is not only bettering yourself, but also gaining security and self-confidence in the process. The communication chapter (1) mentioned "If we limit ourselves to what's given to us, we are at the mercy of other people." But how do we break out of the "box" we are in at work when the boss won't listen or we don't like the work? Education! Go part-time at night, weekends, or take courses online. That way, you've acquired skills so you can find a job you like. It will enhance your life in many immeasurable ways. You will:

- Make wiser decisions
- Have a goal
- Be investing in your future
- Feel more positive about everything
- Have colleagues, relatives, and spouse supporting your efforts.

If you feel high school is enough education then that's fine. Some people need a college degree and still others need multiple degrees. It depends on your motivation, whether you're trying to compensate from childhood and you're an overachiever or simply wanting a particular career. You can be successful at any level because success is defined by the individual, not society.

I have thoroughly enjoyed doing this project. I entitled it "in-your-face" because we need to treat each other better. We need to learn how to express ourselves, to remember common courtesies and to lift others. It's not about competition for first place and how many trophies you've acquired; it's about how many people you can influence positively to help them succeed in life. Then you are a true winner! The point of this book is to make you stronger and improve your Human Relations skills. We've been preaching success throughout this book, but not at all costs. Temper your drive with faith, determination to help others, and humility. A recent *AP* article about Pope Francis says it well, where he was quoted as saying:

"What star have we chosen to follow in our lives?" *"Some stars may be bright, but do not point the way. So it is with success, money, career, honors and pleasures, when these become our lives,"* the pope said, adding that path won't ensure peace and joy.

"Instead of conducting ourselves in coherence with our own Christian faith, we follow the principles of the world, which lead to satisfying the inclinations toward arrogance, the thirst for power and for riches," Francis said. He prayed instead that *"the world makes progress down the path of justice and of peace."* (D'emilio, 2018).

Communicate clearly, expect great things from yourself and others, stick to your values, treat people ethically, keep your self-esteem healthy, and positively reinforce people. Stay motivated and treat others with respect, be emotionally mature, and to resolve conflict deal with it head-on in a controlled manner. Do these things and you'll definitely live a healthier, happier, and more satisfying life. Be successful so you're in a position to lift everyone around you!

Put this book to good use and help make the world and everyone around you better.

See you on down the road to success. Be sure to use your turn signal, don't speed, focus on your driving, be courteous, and don't cut me off on the freeway! If you do cut me off, then you will need to read this book again!

References

D'emilio, F. (2018, January 7). *AP*. Pope on epiphany: don't make money, career your whole life. *Lubbock Avalanche-Journal*, A8.